THE ENNEAGRAM
and
YOUR MARRIAGE

THE ENNEAGRAM *and* YOUR MARRIAGE

A 7-Week Guide to Better Understanding and Loving Your Spouse

Jackie Brewster

BakerBooks

a division of Baker Publishing Group
Grand Rapids, Michigan

© 2023 by Jackie Brewster

Published by Baker Books
a division of Baker Publishing Group
PO Box 6287, Grand Rapids, MI 49516-6287
www.bakerbooks.com

Printed in the United States of America

Library of Congress Cataloging-in-Publication Data
Names: Brewster, Jackie, author.
Title: The enneagram and your marriage : a 7-week guide to better understanding and loving
      your spouse / Jackie Brewster.
Description: Grand Rapids, MI: Baker Books, a division of Baker Publishing Group, [2023] |
      Includes bibliographical references.
Identifiers: LCCN 2022020834 | ISBN 9781540902573 (paperback) | ISBN 9781493439591
      (ebook)
Subjects: LCSH: Marriage—Religious aspects—Christianity—Textbooks. |
      Enneagram—Textbooks.
Classification: LCC BV835 .B678 2023 | DDC 248.8/44—dc23/eng/20220808
LC record available at https://lccn.loc.gov/2022020834

The names and details of the people and situations described in this book have been changed or presented in composite form in order to ensure the privacy of those with whom the author has worked.

Visual illustrations created by Ali Newton-Lopes.

Published in association with The Bindery Agency, www.TheBinderyAgency.com.

Baker Publishing Group publications use paper produced from sustainable forestry practices and post-consumer waste whenever possible.

23   24   25   26   27   28   29   7   6   5   4   3   2   1

For Stephen:
The years build upon each other and time does not still,
yet we continue to evolve and hold space for each other
with love and empathy.

And for my four amazing children—Isaiah, Ashlyn, Hope, and Grace:
You are more precious than you know. My hope is one day
you will all find partners who see, accept, and love all of you.

Contents

Introduction

In the dark of night, when the house was still and the kids were fast asleep, my husband, Stephen, and I were feeling safe and secure in our new home—that is, until the weather warnings began. Our phones began buzzing and blaring about the imminent danger caused by recent rainstorms. The floodwaters were rising at record speed, and anyone within the flood zone needed to take immediate action. We knew we were not in the flood zone, but we weren't sure about the threat of this rising water.

We had moved to the area only a month earlier. After two decades of marriage and more than a dozen moves, we had finally purchased and renovated our dream house. We thought about the space and designed it in our heads day and night. We picked out the colors, floors, fixtures, and furniture to make our home a place where we could find refuge and reprieve. We purposely picked this house because it was in a small community that was quiet and quaint and seemingly posed little threat of danger. We had the house inspected, and it passed with flying colors.

So when the warnings of rising floodwaters began, we believed our new home was safe. In fact, we thought it was so safe that we didn't even get out of bed to check the rise of the water around us. It was not until Stephen went into the garage the next morning that we had any inkling of possible water damage. He had gone out to grab something from the car when he noticed all the empty bins from our move had been knocked over. From there, he saw that the trash had been dumped out of the rather large trash can. After surveying the state of the whole garage, Stephen realized that the water had flooded it by more than seven inches overnight. It had receded by the time he went out there, leaving only clues behind.

We were shocked the water had risen so high but were thankful the house had not been impacted. The garage is lower than the rest of the house, so the flooding only made a small mess and caused the garage refrigerator to stop working temporarily. Luckily we had already unpacked and put away all of our belongings, so we believed we were safe from any significant issues. We went about the next few days without realizing a much bigger issue was brewing beneath the house.

A few days after the warnings had woken us up and the water had receded, our house became very cold. I thought Stephen might have turned the heat off or below my comfort level, which happens quite often, so I texted him to turn the heat up a bit. All day I battled the cold while feeling confused by the temperature situation. After all, the heating unit was relatively new, and we had no reason to believe anything was wrong with it. After a full day of uncomfortably cold temps and a night of shivering, we called in the experts. Within ten minutes of starting his inspection, the service technician came into our house with a look of concern and asked, "Did you know your crawl space flooded thigh high and all your ductwork is underwater?"

In utter shock, all I could say was, "NO." He proceeded to tell me that not only had the ductwork been flooded but so had the entire heating unit. To fix the problem, they would have to replace all of the ductwork and the heating unit and rebuild the foundation the unit sits on so it would not flood in the future. In addition, the ductwork would have to be expanded for optimal airflow and function.

The duct system is what distributes heat and circulates air and keeps the house at a comfortable temperature. Without fixing and replacing the necessary components, the ductwork would push mold, mildew, and other nasty agents into our house and the heating unit would not function properly.

To say Stephen and I were speechless is an understatement. We both looked at the quote and instantly began to feel nauseous and nervous. It was a larger number than we had imagined, and we had just finished renovating this house to be our dream home. We had done all the improvements that made the house look beautiful, warm, and inviting, but this repair that needed to be done was something nobody would ever see. This fix was below the surface but would greatly impact how the home functioned.

The Importance of a Sturdy Foundation

As all of this was transpiring, I couldn't help but think about the way many of us approach dating, relationships, and marriage. We often get caught up in the outward expression of love and miss the depth found in knowing someone for who they are and what has made them into the person they have become. We often project the best version of ourselves in hopes of wooing and winning the person we desire. Our faults and flaws come out much later in the dating relationship, or perhaps not until after the words "I do" are uttered, and by then it feels too late to turn back. We tend to place unspoken expectations on each other, hoping the other person will fulfill our dreams of being the perfect partner and giving us the perfect life. However, as our true colors begin to surface, we may feel duped, vulnerable, exposed, unloved, lonely, alone, abandoned, rejected, or maybe even scared. That is why I believe it is more important to work on the underbelly of the relationship than just what is at the surface.

What we see, feel, or experience at the surface level of a person is called personality. Personality is made up of moods, attitudes, and opinions, and it is most clearly seen when we interact with others. The personality includes patterns of behavior and behavioral characteristics that have been naturally deposited and learned over time. These characteristics distinguish one person from another. When people get caught up in their own personalities, they tend to get lost in a "this is who I am and this is how it should be" mentality. This mentality keeps walls up and defense mechanisms high and causes a lot of havoc within relationships.

The Enneagram and Your Marriage is a workbook that offers a new and innovative approach to relationships. Instead of just assessing whether you and your partner like similar hobbies and enjoy spending time together, it dives into what makes you and your partner who you are. This workbook prompts you to explore why you do what you do and offers you awareness around your patterns of behavior. You will uncover and discover many different components of your personality, and you will be given opportunities to explore what you think about these components and how they serve you in your current relationship and life.

I believe the foundation of a strong and sustainable relationship starts with building a solid infrastructure. When we hear the word *infrastructure*, we often think of the inner workings of a building. If the foundation is not solid, then the building will eventually collapse. The same idea can apply in the business world. It is critical to have the proper infrastructure so that a business or organization has room to grow and expand.

The same principles that we apply to buildings and organizations can also hold true within our relationships and marriages. We must lay a solid foundation to create a long-lasting, deeply connected marriage. Like the story of my family's dream house illustrates, it is not enough to work on the fixtures and furnishings, because when the storms of life appear, we have to make sure that what is below the surface is sustainable.

I would venture to say most people don't necessarily know how to build a solid foundation within their relationships beyond the basic principles of love and commitment. This is where the Enneagram can be transformational, because it goes beyond love and commitment to help you truly understand how your partner functions in all aspects of life. You will uncover and discover patterns of behavior and thought processes that have been established and built upon since as early as age two. If love and commitment are the glue, what you learn about each other through the Enneagram will give that glue its bonding strength.

The Enneagram and My Marriage

My husband and I have been married for over twenty years, and we have learned the hard way about the importance of building a solid infrastructure. We have gone through our fair share of ups and downs within marriage, ministry, and parenting, and it's a wonder our marriage has survived. Through the years we've learned how to fight for each other and for our family by clinging to Jesus, undergoing years of therapy, and spending time learning about each other through the Enneagram system. The Enneagram has been an significant tool for understanding how each of us thinks, feels, and interprets situations, and for helping us recognize our healthy and unhealthy thought patterns and behaviors.

At the beginning of our relationship, we focused on making each other feel accepted, wanted, warm, and safe, much like we did with our home in the story above. We spent very little time asking the hard questions—and, truth be told, I don't think we even knew which hard questions to ask. We were caught up in the romance of new love, and we married pretty fast. We dated long-distance for nine months before we tied the knot, and I moved to Nashville, Tennessee, to join my new husband and start a new life in a new home with a man I honestly knew little about. It makes sense that as an Enneagram Seven I was up for the adventure of a lifetime and jumped into married life with excitement and passion. Stephen is a Three, so he wanted to get married fast and start our life together without a lot of conversation about what that would actually look like. We both believed we had a solid foundation; after all, we loved God and loved each other. Isn't that enough?

Well, through the many years of marriage, I have to say it takes a whole lot more than loving God and loving each other to build a lasting relationship. Those are foundational elements, but they are not the only elements needed for a relationship to stand the test of time with emotional connection and deep-rooted intimacy. I don't know about you, but I don't want to just go through the motions of marriage. I want a marriage that is not only surviving but also thriving.

Over the years, there have been times when Stephen and I have struggled with feeling alone in our relationship and lost within our marriage. We are both resilient and strong-willed people. We both have a desire to fight for connection and are committed to each other through the highs and lows. But how we each handle that fight has been vastly different. Stephen and I were raised in very different homes. He was a pastor's kid who grew up on the mission field with strict guidelines and expectations. I, on the other hand, grew up with a single mother in Massachusetts. To say we have different upbringings is an understatement. My childhood was full of freedom, fun, and adventure. In contrast, Stephen's childhood was much more orderly and strict and involved a lot of travel as well as living abroad.

When I met Stephen, it was love at first sight, and we did have a whirlwind romance that has lasted over twenty years. People ask me, "Would you marry him again knowing what you know now and what the journey together would look like?" My answer is always a resounding yes. I would choose him again and again, and I do choose him every day. He also chooses me again and again. The beauty in choosing each other is that neither of us feels the need to chase or change the other person. Instead, we each allow the other to evolve over time with love, understanding, and respect. I am incredibly grateful for the help we have had during moments, seasons, and years of heartache and hard times. Because of the empathy and compassion that we've learned to have toward each other through the beautiful tool of the Enneagram, and because of the training I've received from Your Enneagram Coach's Beth McCord, my training at Onsite to be an experiential specialist, and several years of Enneagram coaching, I can write this book with an understanding heart and honest awareness of the journey we call marriage.

As you begin to use *The Enneagram and Your Marriage* to help you and your partner uncover and discover many new, interesting, exciting, and at times challenging pieces of each other, be reminded of the love and compassion you need for yourself. The goal of this journey is to enrich your marriage through self-discovery and deeper understanding and awareness of your partner. As you become aware of your behavior patterns, you will also be able to recognize your partner's patterns. This awareness is the beginning of a deep emotional connection and a loving bond that will help you foster more empathy and compassion for each other.

How to Use This Workbook

This book has been intentionally broken down into seven weeks, with each week building upon the previous week's material. As you dig into each chapter, you will explore Enneagram topics that will help you uncover and discover more about yourself and your partner. It is imperative that you not only read all the content for each week but also do the activities provided. You might be wondering why these activities are important. Well, words are abstract and difficult for the brain to retain. Visuals are concrete and more easily remembered. Psychologists call this the *picture superiority effect*. I have heard it said that people retain 80 percent of what they see, 10 percent of what they hear, and 20 percent of what they read. I believe visual aids and prompts will help you to process the information you are learning. They will also enable you to pause and allow yourself to put into practice some of the awareness tools discussed throughout this book.

I am an experiential specialist as well as a certified Enneagram coach. I have been trained through the International Society for Experiential Professionals, where I learned the importance of incorporating experiential practices in the work I do helping people uncover and discover their patterns of behavior using the tool of the Enneagram. I have been trained and certified to utilize many experiential modalities such as art, sculpting, team building, and mindfulness techniques. I have found when my clients are able to participate in an activity such as drawing, imagery, movement, sculpting, or even using props, they are able to see the information they are trying to process in a much clearer way. This is why there are activities each week that allow you to explore the information you are learning through a creative outlet. I encourage you not to skip this step. Instead, spend some time engaging in each activity and allow yourself to remain open to whatever begins to surface. You may see yourself or your partner through a new lens just by slowing down and giving yourself space to really understand what you're reading and how the patterns of behavior that are being unearthed are affecting your relationships and daily living.

If you and your partner do not know your Enneagram type, begin by taking the Narrative Approach Quick Test in appendix A to find your type. If you both already know your type, you can begin in week 1. Each week, approach one topic at a time either together or individually. If you choose to do this individually, make sure to review your answers and talk about the activities together as you do them or at the end of each section before moving on to the next week. This workbook is meant to be done together, so don't miss out on this opportunity for connection and clarity. However, do what works best for you as a couple.

As you go through this workbook, you may want to journal as you uncover and discover things about yourself and your partner. Again, I encourage you to do what works best for you. You and your partner do not have to do the same thing. If one of you likes to journal and the other doesn't, don't force each other to conform. Instead, be open to each other's differences and watch your relationship flourish.

Remember that the key to this Enneagram-centered journey is embracing the information about your types and letting it transform your relationship. In order for information to become transformational, it must be activated. The power that exists from uncovering and discovering parts of yourself and your partner in this workbook will revolutionize your relationship and take it into a deeper and more meaningful commitment. So dig in and allow yourself to truly explore the information you learn about yourself and your partner. Be intentional about answering the questions throughout this workbook truthfully, and hold space for you and your partner to have honest conversations around each topic with compassion and empathy for each other.

During week 1, you and your partner will work on *building the foundation* of your relationship through Enneagram awareness. You will explore an overview of your Enneagram types along with your subtypes and wings. This information will give you a good picture of yourself and your partner. You may choose to take turns reading aloud the description of the other person's Enneagram type and then ask, "Does this feel true to you?" As you read about yourself, it's important to remember that you are not your number. Rather, your number informs you of the patterns of behavior you have developed over the course of your life as you try to keep yourself safe and secure, have your needs met, and receive love and connection. Your Enneagram type is not meant to put you in a box nor is it meant to excuse unhealthy behavior patterns. Instead, awareness around your Enneagram type allows you to recognize your patterns of behavior and begin to pivot and change what is not working for you any longer.

During week 2, you and your partner will *break down barriers* as you begin to process the unconscious childhood message and core fear for each person's Enneagram type. The content you will uncover and discover this week will be revolutionary for your own personal journey toward health and growth, and from there it will transform your relationship. This new awareness will allow you to understand each other's core motivations and why you do what you do. You both will gain knowledge regarding your patterns of behavior that will position you to individually own your responses and reactions in a new way.

During week 3, you and your partner will *grow together* as you explore the heart longing message and core desire for your individual types. You will learn the importance of speaking words that you each need to hear and how this subtle pivot has the potential to change the trajectory of your relationship. The awareness gained this week will help you to communicate in a way that breeds connection and contentment.

During week 4, you and your partner will *level up* as you unpack the triad and stance for your individual types. You will become aware of the ways you have learned to process information and deal with your emotions. You will also likely have a few aha moments as you begin to understand the ways each of you learned early in life how to keep yourselves emotionally safe by withdrawing, asserting yourself, or becoming compliant. This new awareness will enable you to give each other freedom to say what you need to without fearing the other person's response.

During week 5, you and your partner will learn how to *overcome pitfalls* by uncovering the signature sin and specific defense mechanisms for your personality types. This week's content is powerful and impactful. It will give you insight into each other's specific areas of struggle and weakness as well as revealing ways in which you both try to protect and defend yourselves. The things you will learn about yourself and your partner are not meant to cause shame. Rather, they are intended to shine a light on times when you tend to miss the mark and do, think, or feel in a way that causes more harm than good to you and your relationship. This new awareness will empower you and your partner to have open lines of communication around areas of struggle and create healthy boundaries that ensure trust, security, and connection stay intact within your relationship.

During week 6, you and your partner will *build a solid connection* by understanding stress and growth patterns for your types. The knowledge you gain this week will bring understanding, empathy, and compassion into your relationship. Knowing how and why you each function the way you do in times of stress and growth will enable you to recognize when you are in a good place and when you are not. Learning to listen to hear your partner instead of listening to respond will help build trust within your relationship. When you feel safe in your relationship, you are able to live authentically and love from a place of acceptance and celebration.

During week 7, you and your partner will *grow together* through awareness of your connection-based and outlook-based groups. This week's content will deepen your relationship by exploring how you each have protected yourself from disappointment, frustration, rejection, and connection using specific coping strategies according to your Enneagram type. This new awareness will enable each of you to grow in understanding, patience, and love as you begin to see life through the lens of your partner. Your relationship will flourish because you no longer will take offense at your partner's reactions or lack thereof. You'll understand that it is not about you, and you'll allow your partner to continue their own personal journey of deeper self-understanding. As you learn about and accept yourselves, you will be able to accept each other just as you are with love and grace.

Let this book be a tool for you and your partner to hold space for each other as together you explore your Enneagram type and patterns of behavior. Remember that healthy communication requires mutual understanding, respect, and active listening that involves the use of all of your senses, as well as nonverbal communication such as nodding your head, smiling, eye contact, and gentle touch. Active listening is not something that just happens. It takes a conscious decision to understand the messages that the other person is trying to share with you. Active listening requires you to remain neutral and nonjudgmental. This means you are not forming an opinion or taking a side; instead, you are remaining open and understanding. You try to understand the other person's perspective without becoming defensive and thinking you need to take control of the situation. Active listening also means you give the other person time to explore and process what they are feeling and thinking without asking a lot of questions or telling them what they are feeling and thinking.

Remember, your patterns of behavior have been developed from early childhood. You both have been on guard trying to get your needs met, receive love, and keep yourselves safe in this world. As you become more aware of your behavior patterns, you will begin to see just how often they influence your reactions and decisions. Get ready to finally understand why you and your partner are the way you are.

WEEK 1

Building the Foundation

What Is the Enneagram?

It's in understanding yourself deeply that you can lend yourself to another person's circumstances and another person's experiences.

Lupita Nyong'o

As we get started, let's review what the Enneagram is and where it came from. In his book *The Enneagram: A Christian Perspective*, Richard Rohr describes the Enneagram as "a very old typology that describes nine different characters."[1] In the book *The Wisdom of the Enneagram* by Don Richard Riso and Russ Hudson, we learn that this ancient personality typing system was first brought to the United States in the 1970s by the Chilean psychiatrist Claudio Naranjo, who taught the Enneagram in Berkeley, California, and started using Western psychological terms to describe the nine patterns of behavior.[2] The word *Enneagram* comes from the Greek words *ennea*, meaning "nine," and *grammos*, meaning "figure."[3] This refers to the nine-pointed geometric figure—one point for each personality type—that the system was originally based on. Since its introduction in the US, a host of teachers, psychologists, and psychiatrists have refined and expanded it to create today's Enneagram system.

The information in this book is based on years of studying Enneagram books such as *The Wisdom of the Enneagram* by Don Richard Riso and Russ Hudson, *The Complete Enneagram* by Beatrice Chestnut, *The Enneagram: A Christian Perspective* by Richard Rohr, *Self to Lose, Self to Find* by Marilyn Vancil, *The Journey toward Wholeness* by Suzanne Stabile, and many others. It also includes insights I gained from sitting under the teachings of Ian Morgan Cron, Beatrice Chestnut, Russ Hudson, and other great teachers of the Enneagram and earning my certification as an Enneagram coach from Beth McCord of Your Enneagram Coach.

To truly understand your Enneagram type, you need to know more than just your primary number. The Enneagram system is made up of your number, your wing numbers, and your subtype. You also have a stress number that you go to in times of high pressure and unhappiness, and a growth number that you go to in periods of healthy personal growth. If this all sounds complicated, don't worry! Every week we will explore these elements in-depth to help you and your partner gain more knowledge and insight about each other.

Remember, information is not transformation until it becomes activated, so take your time and activate the information you are learning about yourself and your partner by doing the activities offered in each week's teaching. This will allow a true and lasting transformation of your relationship from the ground up.

One more thing before we dive in. While the Enneagram system is a vast and insightful way to learn about yourself—who you are, why you do what you do, how you interact with others—it can be easy to get caught up in the numbers and lingo and forget about this foundational truth: You are an individual who has been uniquely crafted on purpose for a purpose. No matter what Enneagram number you are, you have your own unique life story. Your personality and life experiences have been woven together through behavioral patterns you practice to help get your needs met, receive love, and keep yourself safe. These patterns reveal the true motivation behind why you do what you do.

As you read the descriptions of each Enneagram type below, allow yourself to stay open and curious. Learning about yourself on this journey of self-discovery may be overwhelming and uncomfortable at times. If you feel exposed or vulnerable as you read about your Enneagram number, take some time and ask yourself, "What is making me feel most uncomfortable at this moment?" It may be that as you read about your Enneagram number you finally feel seen and understood for the first time in your life. If that is the case, take some time and ask yourself, "What feelings are surfacing as I finally feel seen and understood?" Make it a point to notice the positive qualities that you exhibit and allow yourself to embrace the good aspects of your Enneagram type. You may even want to make a list of the positive qualities you bring into your relationship so you can better recognize them when they are being displayed.

Learning about yourself through the lens of the Enneagram allows you to accept parts of yourself you may have felt were flawed, broken, or of no value. As you begin to unpack your patterns of behavior, you will start to see where your thoughts, ideas, struggles, strongholds, competence, and confidence (or lack thereof) come from. By allowing yourself to see and explore your life through the Enneagram lens, you have an opportunity to embrace this new awareness that can reshape you and shift your life toward a more positive outlook and a hopeful future.

Overview of the Enneagram Types

The Moral Perfectionist

Triad: Gut

Divine attributes: Goodness and rightness

Core desire: To be seen as good

Signature sin: Anger

Core fear: Being seen as unworthy

Heart longing message: "You are good."

Ones are known for being responsible, compassionate, hardworking people. They have a high moral standard and cannot always understand why others don't feel the same way they do about things. They are ethical and reliable. If they say they are going to do something, you can trust them to follow through. Ones are also great at coming up with plans and procedures. They enjoy a challenge and like to establish order to help accomplish the tasks at hand. Their eyes are naturally drawn to mistakes and mess-ups, and they recognize what is wrong or does not fit. They often see the negative before the positive, and typically they can't help but share their thoughts and opinions about whatever issue is at hand. They are perfectionists in many, but not all, areas of life. At times they may appear rigid or judgmental because of their black-and-white view of the world.

The Supportive Adviser

Triad: Heart

Divine attributes: Love and nurture

Core desire: To be needed, wanted, and loved

Signature sin: Pride

Core fear: Being unwanted

Heart longing message: "You are wanted and loved."

Twos are known for being generous, warm, supportive, and nurturing. They are relationship-driven people who long for deep connection and commitment. They are supportive of others and often will suppress their own needs to give to others as a way of feeling connected, protected, and loved. They have a natural ability to sense others' needs and often try to meet those needs before having a conversation with the person about what they are seeing or sensing. Twos tend to be permissive because they don't like to deal with conflict or anything that will cause separation between them and their partner, children, family, or friends. At times they can become manipulative, bossy, and even demanding if they feel they have been overlooked, underappreciated, undervalued, or excluded. They seek connection through relationships, career success, climbing the corporate ladder, or being the most attractive and desirable person in the room.

The Determined Achiever

Triad: Heart

Divine attribute: Hope

Core desire: To be successful

Signature sin: Deceit

Core fear: Being seen as irrelevant

Heart longing message: "You are loved for who you are."

Threes are known to be driven, optimistic achievers who work hard to accomplish all of their goals. They are function-focused and desire to accomplish tasks, projects, and plans to be the best at what they do. They are incredibly competitive and do not like it when people get in the way of their plans. They tend to have a project-over-people mentality; however, they struggle with people-pleasing, which can cause them to shape-shift in an effort to become what others view as successful and desirable. They are also known to be great encouragers and champions of the people they care about because they want to help their loved ones and friends achieve success. Threes tend to be very image-conscious and superficial at times, even with their partners. When confronted or questioned, their cool, calm demeanor often switches to defensiveness as they try to protect their image.

The Romantic Individualist

Triad: Heart

Divine attributes: Creativity and depth

Core desire: To be seen as unique

Signature sin: Envy

Core fear: Being overlooked or disregarded

Heart longing message: "You are seen and valued for who you are."

Fours are known to be intuitive, expressive, and deeply concerned with authenticity. They pursue their passions with curiosity and an open heart and mind. They desire for all people to be valued, seen, and heard whether they agree with them or not. They are compassionate people who feel deeply and often feel misunderstood. Fours long to be accepted just as they are, and they do not shift and change to meet others' expectations. They can become withdrawn, irritable, and even confrontational if they perceive others are not accepting them. They long for deep connections with people who are open to creative ways of viewing the world. When they are in a relationship and the connection feels faulty, they push their partner away, hoping their partner will chase after them. This can create a cat-and-mouse pattern within the Four's relational expectations.

The Investigative Thinker

Triad: Head

Divine attribute: Wisdom

Core desire: To gather resources and knowledge

Signature sin: Greed

Core fear: Being depleted

Heart longing message: "Your needs are not a problem."

Fives are known to be intellectual thinkers who gather knowledge about many topics, so they are always prepared for whatever may happen. They are witty, insightful, caring people who enjoy a lot of alone time and privacy. They prefer to deal with and feel their emotions privately and do not like to be pushed to share their feelings openly. They tend to get easily overwhelmed when there is a lot of noise and stimulation and need to find a quiet place to retreat and recharge. At times Fives can be cynical, and they may distance themselves from others when they disagree with how a situation is being handled or with the views of the people around them.

The Friendly Loyalist

Triad: Head

Divine attribute: Courage

Core desire: To be certain

Signature sin: Fear

Core fear: Being without support

Heart longing message: "You are safe and secure."

Sixes are known to be trustworthy and loyal people who enjoy being with others and offering their support. They are understanding and kind yet willing to ask hard questions and push on situations to see if people, organizations, and institutions are trustworthy. They love to work alongside other people and are great at seeing the big picture. At times they are overly cautious, which can cause frustration and angst within relationships because they may abruptly pump the brakes on plans. While they tend to be hypervigilant, they can appear controlling and overbearing; however, this stems from a desire to keep themselves and those they care about safe.

The Energetic Enthusiast

Triad: Head

Divine attribute: Joy

Core desire: To be free of limits

Signature sin: Gluttony

Core fear: Being trapped in emotional pain

Heart longing message: "You will be taken care of."

Sevens are known for being fun, energetic, joyful people who are full of ideas and plans. They are great encouragers who have a unique ability to gather people and infuse them with exciting vision and passion to carry out the creative ideas they put together. They have a lot of energy and don't like to miss out on gatherings, parties, or plans of any kind. They stay upbeat and positive in hopes of keeping negativity at bay. They can be impulsive and flighty when they don't allow themselves to process their feelings. They tend to get restless when life becomes too quiet because they don't want to deal with heavy feelings or negative thoughts that may surface if they become still. Sometimes Sevens can appear superficial because they do not wish to engage in deep emotional and personal conversations with others unless they are intimately connected to them.

The Protective Challenger

Triad: Gut

Divine attribute: Strength

Core desire: To be in control

Signature sin: Lust

Core fear: Being taken advantage of

Heart longing message: "You will not be betrayed."

Eights are strong, competent, inspiring people who are full of passion and energy. They are big-picture thinkers who desire to move at a break-neck pace and can't understand why others don't feel the same way. They are resilient and forceful people who want to make a big difference in the world. They are great mentors and leaders who are compassionate and caring, often looking out for the underdog. They can be excessive and controlling, which may cause others to retreat for fear of not meeting the high standards the Eight has set for themselves and everyone else. Eights may appear insensitive because of their unwillingness to openly express their feelings, thoughts, and emotions; however, they are very tenderhearted people who do not want to be exposed, betrayed, or made to look weak or incompetent, so they keep their guard up at all times.

9

The Peaceful Mediator

Triad: Gut

Divine attribute: Peace

Core desire: To be at peace

Signature sin: Sloth

Core fear: Being insignificant

Heart longing message: "Your presence matters."

Nines are known to be calm, caring, and receptive. They like to know that their voice matters and their thoughts and ideas are valued. They are excellent mediators and have a unique ability to see all sides of a situation. They are genuinely kind, accepting, and inclusive people who desire others to be treated fairly in all situations and circumstances. Nines can appear detached because they do not like to deal with conflict of any kind. This does not mean they won't deal with conflict; it's just that they would prefer to avoid conflict because they desire to live in a peaceful and harmonious environment. Nines can become irritable when they feel their voice is not being heard, and they may even erupt if they have been pushed too hard or feel underappreciated or devalued.

Questions

What have I learned about myself from reading my Enneagram description?

Partner 1:

Partner 2:

What does it feel like to have my partner read about me?

Partner 1:

Partner 2:

What part of my Enneagram number's description feels most vulnerable?

Partner 1:

Partner 2:

What strengths does my Enneagram number reveal?

Partner 1:

Partner 2:

—————— Overview of the Three Subtypes ——————

Whether it was someone's reaction to a problem or their decision on how to spend their free time, we have all faced situations where we just could not understand why our loved ones acted in a certain way. What if I told you the confusion probably has something to do with how each of you views the world, how you try to keep yourselves safe, and how you get your needs met? This dissonance can be explained through Enneagram subtypes.

Alicia is a self-preservation Two, and Will is a one-to-one Three. They have a lot in common. They both love to connect with people and help others achieve their goals. They are both very in tune with what others think, feel, and need. From the outside they look like the perfect couple: kind, loving, and supportive of one another. However, behind closed doors Alicia often feels alone and frustrated. She likes the security of her home and the comfort of knowing she has everything she needs to keep herself safe and secure. On the other hand, Will often feels confused and at times even controlled by Alicia's desire to extend her idea of security onto their relationship. He prefers to push the limits and overextends himself because he gets lost in other people's expectations of him, sometimes to the detriment of his marriage. This disconnect has caused a lot of conflict and tension within their relationship.

After Alicia and Will learned about their subtypes, they gained a better understanding of what they needed individually to feel secure not only in their relationship but also in the world. They have been able to communicate their needs, wants, and desires from a place of knowing instead of a place of protection and defense. They no longer allow themselves to believe they are being rejected, abandoned, forgotten, controlled, or held back by the other person. Instead, they now ask to have a clarifying conversation, which allows them to respect what each person needs in each situation that arises.

After you have confirmed your Enneagram number, it is important to look at your number through the lens of the three subtypes. Beatrice Chestnut, a well-known Enneagram teacher, describes the subtypes as "three different 'subsets' of the patterns of the nine types that provide even more specificity in describing the human personality."[4] Subtypes refer to how each Enneagram number has learned to find safety and security when interacting with the world around them. That means each number has three distinct ways in which they appear. We all have one dominant subtype that is used most often. Our secondary subtype becomes activated as we adapt to different situations, and the third subtype is more likely to be repressed.

The subtype you most relate to reveals how you find safety and security in the world—through comfort, connection, or involvement. Subtypes explain how two people can have the same Enneagram type but express the characteristics in different ways. If you and your partner do not have the same subtype, you will likely feel frustrated, misunderstood, confused, lost, or perhaps alone, even if you share the same number. As you read the descriptions of each subtype, think about how the differences could affect the way you and your partner approach everyday life.

Self-preservation subtypes are concerned with safety, security, and comfort. They want to know they have a roof over their head and food on the table. They make their home a warm place and focus on taking care of their physical needs.

Social subtypes are most concerned with having a connection to a core group of people. They believe there is safety in numbers. However, this does not mean they are extroverted. Instead, they focus on finding people to do life with so they know they are safe.

One-to-one subtypes focus on the chemistry between themselves and others. Also called the "intimate" or "sexual" subtype, they are more willing to take risks and are not as concerned with personal safety and security. They will go without eating or caring for their own needs so they won't miss out on whatever is happening in the moment.

Below is a list of all nine Enneagram numbers according to their three distinct subtypes. These subtypes have unique characteristics that will give you a clearer picture of yourself. Unlike your Enneagram type, which does not change, your dominant subtype can adjust and change through the years. All three of your subtypes can be activated in different situations or circumstances. For instance, if self-preservation is your dominant subtype, you may act more reserved when you are at work or out in public. However, if your secondary subtype is one-to-one, you may lean into that part of your personality when your needs are not being met at home.

It is important to remember that identifying your Enneagram number and your subtype does not excuse your acting out unhealthy patterns or behaviors. Instead, as you begin to see yourself with more clarity and compassion, ask yourself questions like "Why do I feel the need to protect myself in this way?" or "How has using this subtype gotten me what I wanted or kept me safe and secure throughout my life?"

Ones focus on perfecting. There are three different ways this can be expressed:

Self-Preservation Ones

- Focus on making everything they do perfect
- Concerned with their health and material well-being
- Have a strong inner critic that sees all their flaws
- Anxious and worried
- Friendly and warm

Social Ones

- Focus on doing things perfectly
- Believe they know the right way things should be done
- Often referred to as a "teacher"
- Intellectual
- Believe it is their role to help people see what they themselves already know

One-to-One Ones

- Focus on making society and other people more perfect
- Reformers

- Do not see their flaws because they are more focused on the flaws of others
- Openly express their anger
- Display enthusiasm about a cause

Twos focus on gaining the approval of others and keeping their relationships positive. There are three different ways this can be expressed:

Self-Preservation Twos

- Youthful and playful
- Repress their own self-preservation needs
- Feel a sense of burden about helping others
- Charm others into liking them as a way of getting people to take care of them
- Fearful and unsure about connecting with others because of possible rejection

Social Twos

- Seek approval of others
- Want to be seen as powerful, competent, and influential
- Strong leaders
- Overextend themselves trying to stay in everyone's good graces
- Can show off while trying to prove their value

One-to-One Twos

- Generous
- Care about personal appearance
- Promise to support others as a way of getting others to do things for them
- More in tune with their emotions
- Passionate

Threes focus on achieving and looking good while they do it. There are three different ways this can be expressed:

Self-Preservation Threes

- Care about material security for themselves and those they care for
- Want to be seen as successful
- Desire to be seen as people of integrity and character
- Do not like to brag or self-promote
- Self-sufficient and result-oriented

Social Threes

- Desire to appear flawless to others
- Competitive
- Materialistic and image-conscious
- Performer
- Highly driven and achievement-oriented

One-to-One Threes

- Create an image that is appealing to others
- Supportive of the people around them
- People-pleasing
- Dazzling and charming
- Work hard to support the success of others above their own

Fours focus on expressing themselves creatively and authentically. There are three different ways this can be expressed:

Self-Preservation Fours

- Long-suffering
- Emotionally sensitive
- Withhold their feelings from others for fear of losing connection
- Feel deeply but have a happy, upbeat disposition
- Not easily frustrated

Social Fours

- In tune with their inner world of emotions
- Compare themselves to others
- Create space for others to engage with feelings and emotions
- Social and engaging
- Care deeply about authenticity

One-to-One Fours

- Assertive
- Competitive
- Openly ask for what they need
- Complain when their needs are not met
- Can be emotionally turbulent

Fives focus on gathering knowledge. They also put boundaries around themselves to keep others from getting too close and invading their private space. There are three different ways this can be expressed:

Self-Preservation Fives

- Focus on maintaining boundaries with others
- Private space is essential
- Focus on having all the resources necessary for survival within reach
- Are less expressive and more introverted
- Enjoy spending time with a few people they trust

Social Fives

- Seek to be experts in a particular field
- Gather knowledge and resources
- Connect with others who have similar interests
- Do not like to share their space, time, or resources with others
- Constantly looking for life's purpose and meaning

One-to-One Fives

- Desire to find a connection with one ideal partner
- Romantic flair
- Socially aware
- Share their desires, hopes, and dreams more openly
- Emotionally in tune but may not show it outwardly

Sixes focus on what could go wrong and how to fix it. They seek safety and security and do not trust easily. There are three different ways this can be expressed:

Self-Preservation Sixes

- Actively fearful
- Phobic
- Question everything to determine how secure they are
- Warm and friendly
- Look to connect with others as a form of support

Social Sixes

- Rule follower
- Intellectual
- Loyal
- Rational
- Care about policies and procedures

One-to-One Sixes

- Strong-willed
- Can appear intimidating to others
- Fight through their fears
- Risk-takers
- Rebellious and at times defensive

Sevens focus on what feels good in the moment. They are always looking for stimulating ideas to distract them from whatever might cause them to feel uncomfortable. There are three different ways this can be expressed:

Self-Preservation Sevens

- Practical
- Recognize opportunities
- Planners
- Networkers
- Talkative, friendly, and self-indulgent

Social Sevens

- Don't want to be seen as excessive or opportunistic
- Desire to be of service to others
- Deny their wants
- Take responsibility for the group
- Overextend themselves

One-to-One Sevens

- Idealistic
- Look for greener grass
- Enthusiastic
- Fickle and fearful of commitment
- Future-oriented thinkers

Eights focus on power, control, and justice. They are big-picture thinkers who are assertive and direct, and there are three different ways this can be expressed:

Self-Preservation Eights

- Go after what they want in a direct way
- No-nonsense
- Easily frustrated

- Care about material possessions
- Business savvy

Social Eights

- Protective of those they care about
- Enjoy mentoring others
- Can be assertive and rebellious
- Less aggressive than the other two subtypes
- Softer side toward those they care about

One-to-One Eights

- Strong rebellious tendencies
- Desire to be the center of attention
- Like to be in control
- Strong leadership ability
- Can provoke others to anger

Nines focus on creating peace and harmony. They like to go with the flow, hoping to maintain positive feelings and avoid conflict. There are three different ways this can be expressed:

Self-Preservation Nines

- Find comfort in familiar routines
- Desire to have their physical needs met
- Enjoy the comfort of their home
- Lose themselves in activities that help them feel grounded and comfortable
- Merge with others for comfort and support

Social Nines

- Work hard to support the group they are a part of
- Seek comfort and belonging with others

- Desire to be a part of something
- Lighthearted and fun
- Go to great lengths hoping to find acceptance within the community or group

One-to-One Nines

- Merge with others' ideas, attitudes, and beliefs
- Sweet, gentle, and less assertive
- Relationship-oriented
- Take on the feelings and opinions of those close to them
- Desire autonomy and connection at the same time

Questions

As you review your Enneagram number and the three subtypes for your number, write them in order.

Partner 1:

    Dominant:

    Secondary:

    Repressed:

Partner 2:

    Dominant:

    Secondary:

    Repressed:

Why did you put your subtypes in this order?

    Partner 1:

    Partner 2:

Write in your own words how you have sought safety and security in the world.

    Partner 1:

    Partner 2:

    Write down three ways you can better support, protect, and love one another now that you understand each other's subtypes.

    Partner 1:

    Partner 2:

How have your subtypes caused tension and frustration within your relationship?

Partner 1:

Partner 2:

—————— Overview of Enneagram Wings ——————

When Abigail, a Six with a strong Seven wing, started dating Jacob, she was convinced he was a Two. After all, he was kind, generous, thoughtful, and driven. Jacob had all the characteristics she believed a Two possessed, so she was shocked to find out he was actually a Three. She was unaware of how the wings—the numbers to the right and left of your main number—impact the ways each Enneagram type acts. Come to find out, Jacob has a strong Two wing, and because of this he tends to be more people-focused and relationship-oriented. In the past, Abigail had dated a Three who was task-oriented, image-conscious, and tended to be a workaholic. She only knew this type of Three and assumed all Threes behaved the same way. She did not know how much the Four wing played a part in her previous boyfriend's personality, and that is why he and Jacob seemed so different.

As Abigail continued dating Jacob and later married him, she recognized just how much the Three personality was his driving force. He is incredibly driven, competent, and can easily adapt to his environment, much like a Three, but because he has a strong Two wing, he is able to move from function mode to supportive mode a little bit easier than a Three with a Four wing.

For Abigail and Jacob, understanding how their wings play a part in rounding out their personality has had a huge impact on the way they communicate with each other. It has also helped them talk about what healthy expectations look like within their own skill sets. They no longer misread each other's bids for connection or dismiss each other when they feel misunderstood or undervalued. Instead, they use the skills and understanding they have learned through Enneagram awareness to speak the truth in love with one another.

· · · · · ·

Remember that your Enneagram type never changes. It functions as the foundation of your personality because it is formed and established in early childhood. The wing numbers are those to the immediate right and left of your primary number, both of which can influence the characteristics of your particular type. I like to think of the wing numbers as the wings of a bird that enable it to fly. Every person usually has a dominant wing and a secondary wing. You will see more characteristics being used from one of the wings than the other, but you can learn to access the positive qualities of both wings in order to become a healthier version of yourself.

As you review each Enneagram wing, take notice of which one you most align with. Remember, there is no right or wrong wing, just like there is no good or bad Enneagram number. Allow yourself to see which wing has had the most influence in your life and has helped to round out your personality.[5]

> **Ones** are the Moral Perfectionists of the Enneagram. They lean more toward either the Nine wing (Peaceful Mediator) or the Two wing (Supportive Adviser). If you are a One, which of these most resonates with you?
>
> - 1w9 (the Idealist): This combination tends to be cooler, more laid back, introverted, objective, and detached.
> - 1w2 (the Advocate): This combination tends to be warmer, more helpful, critical, vocal, sensitive, action-oriented, and controlling.
>
> **Twos** are the Supportive Advisers of the Enneagram. They lean more toward either the One wing (Moral Perfectionist) or the Three wing (Determined Achiever). If you are a Two, which of these most resonates with you?

- 2w1 (the Servant): This combination tends to be more idealistic, reasonable, objective, self-critical, quietly serving, and judgmental.
- 2w3 (the Host): This combination tends to be more self-assured, charming, ambitious, outgoing, and competitive.

Threes are the Determined Achievers of the Enneagram. They lean more toward either the Two wing (Supportive Adviser) or the Four wing (Romantic Individualist). If you are a Three, which of these most resonates with you?

- 3w2 (the Star): This combination tends to be charming, more encouraging, sociable, popular, and attention-seeking.
- 3w4 (the Professional): This combination tends to be focused on work, intellectual, withdrawn, intense, observant, and repressed.

Fours are the Romantic Individualists of the Enneagram. They lean more toward either the Three wing (Determined Achiever) or the Five wing (Investigative Thinker). If you are a Four, which of these most resonates with you?

- 4w3 (the Aristocrat): This combination tends to be more extroverted, upbeat, ambitious, emotionally volatile, concerned with image, and flamboyant.
- 4w5 (the Bohemian): This combination tends to be more introverted, withdrawn, observant, intellectual, and prone to negative emotions.

Fives are the Investigative Thinkers of the Enneagram. Either they lean more toward the Four wing (Romantic Individualist), or they lean more toward the Six wing (Friendly Loyalist). If you are a Five, which of these most resonates with you?

- 5w4 (the Pioneer): This combination tends to be more creative, authentic, sensitive, empathetic, withdrawn, and self-absorbed.
- 5w6 (the Problem Solver): This combination is more extroverted, loyal, anxious, skeptical, cautious, and analytical.

Sixes are the Friendly Loyalists of the Enneagram. They lean more toward either the Five wing (Investigative Thinker) or the Seven wing (Energetic Enthusiast). If you are a Six, which of these most resonates with you?

- 6w5 (the Defender): This combination tends to be introverted, prepared, cautious, anxious, focused, and standoffish.
- 6w7 (the Buddy): This combination tends to be extroverted, materialistic, sociable, playful, funny, energetic, active, and impulsive.

Sevens are the Energetic Enthusiasts of the Enneagram. They lean more toward either the Six wing (Friendly Loyalist) or the Eight wing (Protective Challenger). If you are a Seven, which of these most resonates with you?

- 7w6 (the Entertainer): This combination tends to be loyal, endearing, responsible, outgoing, relationship-oriented, playful, childlike, and anxious.
- 7w8 (the Realist): This combination tends to be carefree, passionate, adventurous, strong, intense, quick-minded, creative, and in charge.

Eights are the Protective Challengers of the Enneagram. They lean more toward either the Seven wing (Energetic Enthusiast) or the Nine wing (Peaceful Mediator). If you are an Eight, which of these most resonates with you?

- 8w7 (the Maverick): This combination tends to be extroverted, enterprising, energetic, quick, materialistic, power-conscious, and egocentric.
- 8w9 (the Bear): This combination tends to be mild-mannered, gentle, receptive, and people-oriented. They are quietly strong, and they enjoy their comforts.

Nines are the Peaceful Mediators of the Enneagram. They lean more toward either the Eight wing (Protective Challenger) or the One wing (Moral Perfectionist). If you are a Nine, which of these most resonates with you?

- 9w8 (the Comfort Seeker): This combination tends to be outgoing, assertive, and antiauthoritarian, and may fluctuate between passive and aggressive.
- 9w1 (the Dreamer): This combination tends to prize integrity and be orderly, idealistic, emotionally controlled, and compliant.

As you ponder your Enneagram number and how the wings have shaped your personality over the years, allow yourself to embrace the positive traits you have developed and take stock of the negative tendencies you may display. The gift of Enneagram awareness is that you don't have to put the labels of your Enneagram number on you like sticky notes; instead, pull the sticky notes off and look at the labels with curiosity while asking yourself these questions: "Where did these behaviors and traits come from?" "Why do I use these traits and behaviors?" "Are these traits and behaviors giving me what I want in my life?"

The sticky note activity below allows you to engage creatively with the information you are learning about yourself. You will be more likely to remember what you write down in this activity versus just making a list in your head. According to Dr. Lynell Burmark, an education consultant who writes and speaks about visual literacy, "unless our words, concepts, ideas are hooked onto an image, they will go in one ear, sail through the brain, and go out the other ear."[6]

Activity

On the sticky note images below, write the dominant attributes you relate to for your Enneagram number. Spend some time thinking through what motivates your behavior in relation to those attributes. For example, as a Nine you might write down the word *Peacekeeper* and go on to explain your motivation for keeping the peace as "a strong need to avoid chaos because it causes me to feel anxious and afraid." Understanding your motivations allows you to begin to see when you are functioning from a place of fear and stress versus a place of understanding and growth.

Partner 1   Partner 2

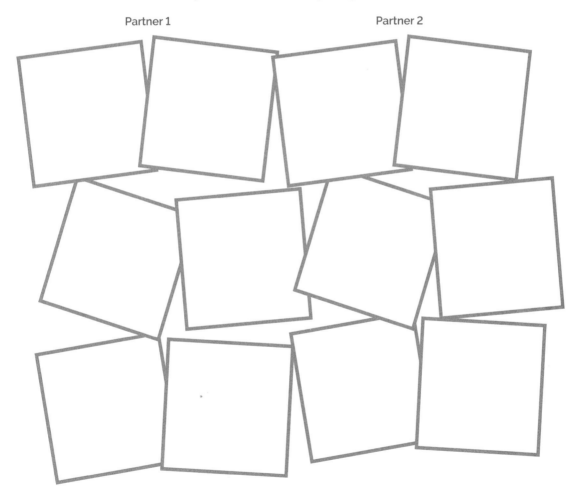

Questions

What are a few of your favorite characteristics of your partner?

Partner 1:

Partner 2:

As you process how your behaviors and traits impact your relationship, write down the ways you have witnessed your traits causing conflict and disconnection in your relationship.

Partner 1:

Partner 2:

What are the traits that you consider beneficial for the health and growth of your relationship?

Partner 1:

Partner 2:

Write down three ways your partner can show they care for you. For example, "I like it when you take a walk with me" or "I like it when you ask me questions about my day."

Partner 1:

1. _____

2. _____

3. _____

Partner 2:

1. _____

2. _____

3. _____

WEEK 2

Breaking Down Barriers

Unconscious Childhood Messages and Core Fears

Life can only be understood backwards, but it must be lived forwards.

Søren Kierkegaard

So much of your childhood has shaped the adults you and your partner are today. Whether you had the perfect childhood or one that you would rather forget, you must look back because of the knowledge that exists in the shadows regarding your familiar patterns of behavior. After all, you can't change what you are unwilling to acknowledge. Over the course of your life, you have gained wisdom by learning what is right and wrong for you and what common sense looks like as it pertains to your goals and relationships. Activating that wisdom takes acknowledging why you keep doing what you're doing even if you're not getting the results you desire.

If you haven't spent some time processing the experiences that have shaped who you are today, you might be at a loss in some areas regarding your relationship. Or if you have tried to push your past to the side, hoping to avoid or ignore the difficult parts, you might be unaware of how this is impacting your relationship in a negative way. The truth is, the elements that make up who you are today have a way of eventually showing up no matter how hard you try to avoid or ignore them. You will see the effects of your childhood experiences in your behavior patterns, decision-making, and ability or inability to emotionally connect with your partner.

The Enneagram system gives you words to help describe how you have felt since early childhood. It's called the *unconscious childhood message*. In their book *The Wisdom of the Enneagram*, Don Richard Riso and Russ Hudson explain where the unconscious childhood message comes from: "We all received many different unconscious messages from our mother and father during childhood. Those messages had a profound effect on our growing identity and on how much we were allowed to fully be ourselves."[1] They also establish a healthy understanding that these messages do not reflect poor parenting but instead give us a better picture that "even in the best circumstances, our parents inevitably could not meet all of our developmental needs perfectly."[2]

Perhaps at some point you've thought, "There is something fundamentally wrong with me." Riso and Hudson suggest that we all internalize a message that leaves us feeling exposed in a particular way: "Even if we cannot express it in words, we feel the tug of a powerful, unconscious anxiety—our Basic Fear."[3] Each Enneagram type has an unconscious childhood message and a core fear that are key motivators and greatly shape our patterns of behavior.

Dr. Sue Johnson, a clinical psychologist and one of the developers of emotionally focused therapy for couples, writes, "From the earliest days, our brain grows and develops in response to our love relationships. . . . Our early relationships build the brain, literally."[4] As you begin to unpack your Enneagram type's unconscious childhood message, you will understand just how important your early childhood life experiences truly are. You will begin to see how they have been the driving force behind your motivations your entire life.

Your number's core fear is directly tied to your unconscious childhood message. Your core fear greatly impacts your patterns of behavior—after all, you want to keep yourself safe and avoid feelings of shame, rejection, abandonment, and defeat. You have learned to adapt to life by allowing your unconscious childhood messaging to inform you of what you need to guard against and why and when to be hypervigilant. You have tried to protect yourself from anything or anyone that could cause a potential threat.

——— Dealing with Unconscious Childhood Messages ———

Scott, a Three, and Julie, a Seven, have been married for just over twelve years. They have four children: a nine-year-old son, a seven-year-old daughter, and two-year-old twin daughters. Having four children under the age of ten has been chaotic, crazy, fun, and intense. Before Scott and Julie knew about the Enneagram or had gone through any counseling, they were hanging on by a thread and a prayer. Within the hectic nature of their lives, they did not understand why they often felt triggered by each other. Using certain words or phrases, facial expressions, body language, or even their avoidant behaviors would activate negative reactions from one spouse to the other.

There was one instance when Julie called Scott a couple of weeks before Easter to let him know she needed to buy the twins shoes for their outfits. He let out a big sigh, which spiraled Julie into one of her biggest fears. As a Seven, Julie had lived her life believing "It's not okay to depend on anyone for anything." Scott's sigh caused Julie to go straight into survival mode. She immediately got off the phone and started thinking frantically about how she could make money to support herself and the kids. Because of her unconscious childhood messaging, she felt very strongly that her husband didn't want to financially support her and the kids in any way.

When Scott came home that evening, he was confused to be met with sadness and anger at the door. Julie had always been the pursuer in their relationship, and Scott had typically been the one to withdraw and retreat to avoid conflict, emotionally charged conversations, and frustration. Julie needed Scott at that moment to comfort her and tell her he loved her and the kids. But as a Three, Scott's unconscious childhood message was "It's not okay to have your own feelings and identity."

As he tried to process what he had done to make Julie feel this way, his own defenses went up. He thought he had done the right thing by putting money in the account for her to buy the shoes. He had no clue she had mistaken his sigh as frustration about providing for her and the children.

In reality, his sigh was simply frustration that he had to do the same task twice. His unconscious childhood messaging was also triggered, and he began to think "It's never good enough" and "I am never good enough."

Scott was fighting the feeling that he should just walk away. Instead, he looked at Julie and said, "I know the girls needed shoes. It is my joy to provide for you and the kids. I had just transferred money before you called, so I was going to have to do it again, and I hate doing the same task twice." Julie calmed down after hearing Scott say these words. She could see how her unconscious childhood messaging had caused her to go into panic mode, trying to find ways to protect herself. Scott also understood his unconscious childhood messaging had kicked in and thrown him into defense mode.

They both were able to process this scenario through the lens of the Enneagram. They now understood the importance of slowing down the situation and asking questions like "Is it true?" "Does my partner really think this way?" and "Is that what they really said, or is that my interpretation of what they said?" Because of the awareness they had gained around unconscious childhood messaging, they could have empathy and compassion toward one another instead of immediately going into defense mode and being concerned only with protecting themselves and their story.

* * * * * *

Your unconscious childhood message causes your core fear to be triggered and your defense mechanism to be activated. Once activated, your body will go into fight-or-flight mode, and from there you will begin to act out your relationship cycle. Les Greenberg, who developed emotionally focused therapy, describes this cycle as one person being the "pursuer" and the other being the "distancer" or the withdrawer in the relationship.[5]

These relationship cycles are tied to early childhood because they reflect how you learned to deal with conflict and stress in your environment when you were young. If you learned the best way to deal with difficult conversations was to avoid and retreat, you likely still do that today. If you learned it was best to talk it out and get some sort of resolution so you could calm yourself down, then you likely try to have the conversation or even engage in the fight because the silence is too scary.

Unconscious Childhood Message

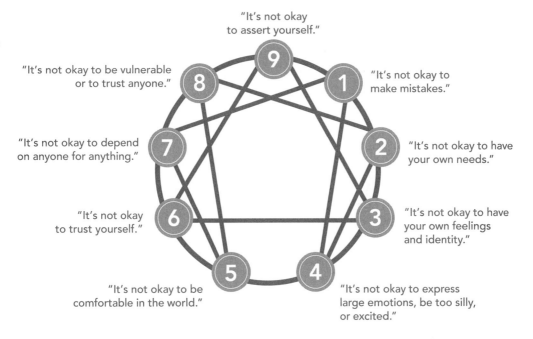

"It's not okay
to assert yourself."

"It's not okay to be vulnerable
or to trust anyone."

"It's not okay to
make mistakes."

"It's not okay to depend
on anyone for anything."

"It's not okay to have
your own needs."

"It's not okay
to trust yourself."

"It's not okay to have
your own feelings
and identity."

"It's not okay to be
comfortable in the world."

"It's not okay to express
large emotions, be too silly,
or excited."

Adapted from Don Richard Riso and Russ Hudson, *The Wisdom of the Enneagram* (New York: Bantam Books, 1999), 31.

The relationship cycle presents in three specific ways. The first is when one partner pursues while the other partner withdraws. This may look like one partner trying to engage in conversation and the other partner not making eye contact, not verbally responding, and/or physically removing themself from the situation. The second type of relationship cycle is when both partners pursue. It can feel intense and volatile at times because both partners are willing to come to the table and fight it out. The fighting might escalate, and they both may need time to cool down before they can come to a resolution. The third type of relationship cycle is when both partners withdraw, and on the surface it appears quiet and distant. It might seem great that no one is getting heated and there is no fighting or conflict. However, this cycle is the most dangerous because when neither partner feels safe or listened to or supported enough to bring up something that is bothering them, emotional distance is created within the relationship.

Healthy emotional connection is necessary for a marriage to be able to withstand the many challenges a couple faces through the years. Emotional connection requires respectful and open communication, eye contact, and the ability to engage in a variety of conversations. Whichever relationship cycle you and your partner currently engage in, know it will be greatly impacted by the Enneagram awareness work you both are doing. Understanding the unconscious childhood messaging your partner struggles with gives you insight into what could be the cause of the conflict. You can learn to communicate and connect with each other and slow down the cycle by practicing active listening, making a conscious effort to hear not only the words the other person is saying but, more importantly, the complete message being communicated. Once you understand your Enneagram type's unconscious childhood message, you will be able to see the root cause of most of your fights. Then, instead of pursuing or withdrawing to try and protect yourself, you can choose to have calm conversations that seek emotional connection.

Here's an example of what a healthy conversation and connection might look like.

Ben, an Eight, was trying to explain why he had decided to buy a new car without even mentioning it to his wife, Sara, who is a Two. Trying to gain understanding, Sara asked Ben if he thought that was a wise decision. After all, they had some rather large expenses coming up with one of their children graduating high school and going off to college. Feeling frustrated and perhaps a little exposed or foolish, Ben started to raise his voice at his wife, and in response Sara shrank back and began to withdraw. Ben quickly recognized what was happening and chose to move toward Sara and hug her. He apologized for his strong reaction and said, "I think my unconscious childhood messaging was triggered. I know you weren't trying to embarrass me or make me feel stupid. You were just trying to understand my decision." Sara responded by holding Ben and affirming him, and she asked if in the future she could be involved with making the decision for purchases of this size.

Awareness will enable you to make decisions that move you and your partner toward each other instead of continuing patterns of behavior that no longer serve you and cause frustration and friction within your relationship.

Activity

The images below represent the three unique relationship cycles: pursue/pursue, pursue/withdraw, and withdraw/withdraw. As you consider these images, discuss with your partner which cycle you most often end up in and write your names in the circles that best reflect the roles you each play.

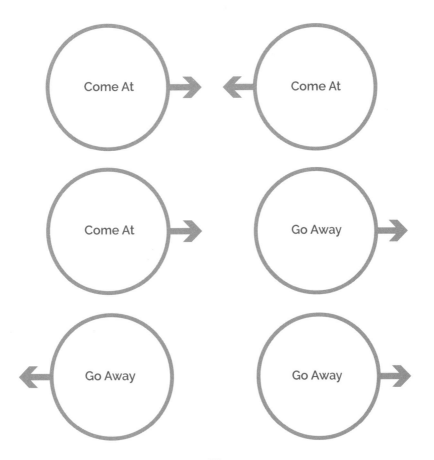

Spend some time talking about why you take on that particular role and see if you can trace back some of the behavior patterns to your early coping strategies. Next, come up with a plan of action that can help you both recognize when you're stepping into your relationship cycle and how you can practice active listening to help grow your marriage toward a deeper emotional connection.

Remember, your unconscious childhood message leaves a silent wound within you. Even though you may not be aware of this message, we all move through life either trying to prove it isn't true or fearing that it is. When you guard yourself and put walls up around the wound this message created, you will struggle to pursue the very things your heart longs for: connection, a sense of belonging, and an emotionally strong relationship. So remember that the triggering reactions between you and your partner may be a sign that you are trying to protect yourself to avoid any more unconscious childhood wounding. But what you both desperately crave is connection.

Below is a phrase for each Enneagram type that helps repair its unconscious childhood message. Locate your partner's phrase and begin to incorporate that message through actions, conversations, and intentional connection.

One: My love for you is not tied to your being perfect.

Two: My love for you is not tied to how you take care of me.

Three: My love for you is not dependent on what you can offer me.

Four: My love for you is not dependent on your being even-tempered and reserved.

Five: My love for you is not dependent on your ability to be overly social or excitable.

Six: My love for you is not attached to your ability to suppress your anxieties and fears.

Seven: My love for you is not dependent on your ability to be independent and adventurous.

Eight: My love for you is not attached to your success or status.

Nine: My love for you is not dependent on your keeping the peace.

I encourage you to take some time this week and process your unconscious childhood message. Engaging in the following activity will enable you to take the information you have learned this week and begin to understand the many ways that message has impacted your patterns of behavior as well as the ways it has influenced your thoughts and reactions.

Activity

Each of you write the unconscious childhood message for your Enneagram number on the line above your circle.

Inside your circle, write how you have learned to keep yourself safe, receive love, and get your needs met throughout your life by using the lens of your unconscious childhood messaging.

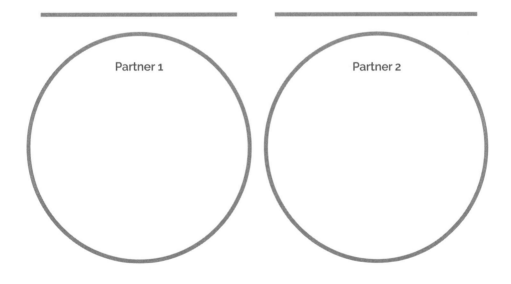

Questions

Can you trace your unconscious messaging back to a particular person or situation? If so, who or what?

Partner 1:

Partner 2:

What emotions surface as you read your unconscious childhood message?

Partner 1:

Partner 2:

How have you witnessed your unconscious childhood message causing conflict in your relationships?

Partner 1:

Partner 2:

What are some more productive ways you can help your partner feel loved, valued, and wanted now that you know their unconscious childhood message?

Partner 1:

Partner 2:

───── Uncovering Core Fears and Fear Responses ─────

Lydia and Alec have been married for just under a year. They'd had an on-again, off-again relationship for over four years before Alec got down on one knee and proposed to Lydia in front of her family and friends. Even though they enjoyed each other's company and desired to be together, they often fought about meaningless things and struggled to express what they needed from each other. But instead of giving up, they decided to explore their personality types to see if they could get to the root cause of the fighting before they either moved on or decided to tie the knot.

So Lydia, a Two, decided to do her work first. She had always struggled with expressing her needs. Growing up, she would experience love and acceptance by being what her parents needed her to be and acting in a way that fit with their expectations. Eventually Lydia recognized that her heart longing to be wanted and loved caused her to fear being unloved, unwanted, overlooked, and rejected. This fear caused Lydia to develop patterns of behavior that involved pleasing people and not upholding her boundaries. When Lydia's patterns were not acknowledged or valued, it would trigger her fear of being unloved or unwanted, and she would start a fight or withdraw from Alec. When Lydia became more aware of the way she tried to get her heart longing message met through people-pleasing and ignoring her own needs, she started to understand her own story. She began to tell Alec, "I would like to connect with you because I am feeling like I need to know you love me and want to be with me." This helped Alec understand her needs and begin to meet them.

When Alec, a Three, started exploring the traits of his type, he began to understand that when things got tense, he suppressed negative emotions and adapted to what was expected of him because he did not believe it was okay for him to have his own feelings and identity. Alec began to see the many ways he repressed his emotions and tried to become whatever he felt was valuable in the moment. Looking back on his childhood, he began to understand his heart longing message and the ways he tried to get love and attention from his parents. Alec's parents put a high priority on success and winning, so he gained their affection, affirmation, and attention by achieving athletic and academic success. He knew if he did a good job, his parents would be proud of him. However, when Alec failed, he would withdraw from people because he feared being seen as worthless. He really wanted to know he would be loved for simply being himself, but he had a hard time believing that could actually be true. Alec started seeing his need to always perform or be seen in a good light as a form of self-protection. He started to understand that Lydia wasn't attacking or belittling him when she pointed something out or had a question about something he did. She simply wanted to have a conversation about something she could not relate to or understand. Alec learned to listen to Lydia from a place of security before reacting out of frustration and self-protection.

Lydia and Alec have learned to listen to each other instead of trying to fix each other or the situation, and they recognize the importance of pausing before they respond. They both have a new awareness of each other's core fear and can be careful not to trigger each other but instead demonstrate support and love for one another.

Core Fears

Each Enneagram type has a specific core fear that influences behaviors and reactions. Ignoring the presence of that fear is detrimental to your self-awareness and limits potential growth within your relationship. When partners don't talk about their core fears, they may have negative reactions to certain encounters and comments without realizing what triggered them.

By using the Enneagram as a tool for self-awareness, relational awareness, and growth, you will begin to see the motivations behind your behaviors and how they are directly connected to each type's core fear. Understanding this along with each type's unconscious childhood message is so important to the foundational work of Enneagram awareness. Gaining this awareness enables you to find out why you do certain things, which positions you to gain better control over your patterns of behavior.

Before we get into the specific core fears, it is important to understand that the concepts of trust and mistrust are learned during the first two years of life. As early as age two, we begin developing patterns of behavior to get our needs met, to get what we want, and to keep ourselves safe. John Bowlby, the founder of attachment theory, teaches that how our parents were able to meet our basic needs as infants—such as feeding, changing, nurturing, caring for, and snuggling us—speaks to the adults we become.[6] Over the years we learned what was acceptable and unacceptable within our family unit by our parents' responses to our actions. We also learned how to get attention and affection from our parents through our behaviors.

We're all familiar with the saying "Negative attention is better than no attention." This is clear in the childhood patterns of behavior we see within the Enneagram system. Every child needs love, nurture, attention, and acceptance. Children look to their parents and other significant adults in their lives to know how they should think and feel about themselves. For example, when a child walks into a room and their parent greets them with a big smile and a joyful hello, the child knows they are welcomed and wanted in the space. They take that information inside themselves and think, "I am special to this person and they are happy to see me, which must mean I am important." Now, if a child walks into the same room and the parent doesn't acknowledge the child's presence or perhaps starts pointing out what is wrong with the child, the child would take that information inside themselves differently. Perhaps they would think thoughts like "I am not welcome here," " I don't matter," "I am a mistake," "I am a bad person," or even "I am not worth loving."

As an adult, we also form opinions about ourselves by the way people react and respond to us. In her book *Love Sense*, Dr. Sue Johnson points out, "As we mature, our brain actively works to fasten us to our loved ones."[7] As you can imagine, this plays a large role in your relationship with your partner. How you acknowledge, celebrate, and affirm each other helps you both feel safe and secure within your relationship. And when you both feel safe and secure, you're able to let your guard down and share your core fears without feeling insecure or afraid of rejection or abandonment.

Before we get into the specific fears for each Enneagram type, let's take stock of how to recognize fear-related responses. When you are in a situation that activates your core fear, whether that's a physical encounter or a simple conversation, your body goes into self-protection mode. This is expressed in one of four ways: *fight, flight, freeze,* or *fawn.*[8]

A **fight response** is used to maintain power and control in uncomfortable and dangerous situations. Those who respond this way believe they can keep themselves safe and get their needs met through expressing anger, irritation, frustration, and perhaps even rage. Fight might look like:

Yelling at your partner

Aggressive behavior

Withholding connection from your partner

Talking negatively about your partner to others

A **flight response** is characterized by a desire to get out of uncomfortable or dangerous situations. Those who respond this way withdraw and retreat to escape any pain or emotional turmoil they feel. Flight might look like:

Walking away from your partner

Taking long walks or drives by yourself

Staying at work longer to avoid the tension at home

Putting on music, TV, or a podcast to drown out the tension

A **freeze response** might look like a person's brain has hit the Pause button or is shutting down instead of reacting during an uncomfortable situation. Those who respond this way may appear detached or even unmoved but are actually stuck in a state of hypervigilance, trying to determine whether fight or flight would be better for their safety and well-being. Freeze might look like:

Paralysis

Inner panic

Mentally checking out

Physically stoic behavior

A **fawn response** is activated when a person tries to please or accommodate themselves out of an uncomfortable situation. It might look like being overly available or agreeable, or like not enforcing boundaries. Fawn might look like:

Ignoring your own needs

Praising and affirming your partner even if they are criticizing you

Suppressing your desires

People-pleasing

Earlier this week we explored how the core fears for each Enneagram type are closely tied to that type's unconscious childhood message. Just as those messages can direct the choices we make, the core fears describe the feelings each number seeks to avoid at all costs, which in turn explains some of their common behaviors.

It is important for both partners to understand each other's core fears. When your core fears are activated, it causes each of you to withhold parts of yourself from the other and from the world. As you continue to learn more about each other and extend empathy and compassion to one another, you both will feel safer and more secure in your relationship.

Below is a list of the core fears for each Enneagram type. Take a few minutes and consider the core fears for your number. Allow yourself to acknowledge what fears arise for you, and check the boxes accordingly. You can't change what you are unwilling to acknowledge, so it is important to recognize what you fear and why.

Ones fear being seen as bad, unqualified, irresponsible, wrong, or corrupt in any way.

☐ I fear being seen as corrupt.

☐ I fear making a mistake.

☐ I fear showing anger.

☐ I fear being wrong or inappropriate.

☐ I fear being seen as unqualified or irresponsible.

Twos fear being seen as overly needy and being unwanted, unloved, or separated from others.

☐ I fear being unloved or unwanted.

☐ I fear being overlooked.

☐ I fear not being appreciated.

☐ I fear being rejected or abandoned.

☐ I fear being seen as needy.

Threes fear being seen as incompetent, without value, undesirable, or unmasked.

☐ I fear being seen as a failure.

☐ I fear being seen as incapable or unimpressive.

☐ I fear being second best.

☐ I fear not being able to contribute.

☐ I fear being seen as unworthy of love.

Fours fear being seen as ordinary, living a life without meaning, and being abandoned or rejected.

☐ I fear being seen as too much.

☐ I fear being emotionally cut off.

☐ I fear being abandoned.

☐ I fear being seen as flawed or defective.

☐ I fear not being my authentic self.

Fives fear unclear expectations and being overwhelmed or intruded upon.

☐ I fear having obligations put on me.

☐ I fear being intruded upon.

☐ I fear not knowing enough.

☐ I fear being overwhelmed.

☐ I fear being forced to engage in social activities.

Sixes fear being without support, security, or guidance, and feeling unsafe or exposed.

☐ I fear feeling uncertain.

☐ I fear being involved in chaos.

☐ I fear not having guidance or support.

☐ I fear being blamed or targeted.

☐ I fear being physically abandoned.

Sevens fear being stuck, overwhelmed, and disappointed.

☐ I fear being limited or bored.

☐ I fear feeling inferior.

☐ I fear missing out on something.

☐ I fear feeling disappointed.

☐ I fear being trapped in emotional pain.

Eights fear being seen as vulnerable, powerless, or weak.

☐ I fear being weak or feeling powerless.

☐ I fear being underestimated.

☐ I fear being humiliated.

☐ I fear being controlled or manipulated.

☐ I fear being at the mercy of injustice.

Nines fear being overwhelmed by conflict or not having peace.

☐ I fear being involved in conflict.

☐ I fear not having love and support.

☐ I fear being overlooked or feeling inferior.

☐ I fear not being heard.

☐ I fear being thought of as demanding.

As you process your Enneagram type's core fear, look below at the list of things each type doesn't share with the world. Put a check mark next to the statements you feel are true about you. In the open space, write a sentence about what you would like your partner to know. For example, "I am very self-critical, so when you point out what I have done wrong, it makes me want to scream, cry, retreat, hide . . . "

Parts of myself I don't share with the world as a One:

☐ I am very self-critical.

☐ I often feel lonely.

☐ I struggle with feeling alienated by others.

☐ I often see myself as the only adult in the room.

☐ I feel my way is the right way and have a hard time delegating.

☐ At times I struggle with feelings of depression.

☐ My inner critic can become so overbearing that I constantly beat myself up, even though no one would know this from looking at me.

Parts of myself I don't share with the world as a Two:

☐ I struggle with feelings of loneliness.

☐ I feel like others don't always want me around.

☐ I feel I need to go over and above in helping others so they will want me.

☐ I sometimes feel unappreciated and rejected.

☐ When I am told I have not responded appropriately, I feel an immense amount of shame.

☐ I desperately need to be affirmed by those around me.

Parts of myself I don't share with the world as a Three:

☐ I struggle to see myself as worthy of love.

☐ I am afraid if others do not think I am talented or attractive, they will reject and abandon me.

☐ I fear becoming irrelevant and being tossed to the side.

☐ I keep my need for support and intimacy to a minimum so I don't appear needy.

☐ I struggle with insecurity and emotional vulnerability.

☐ I often feel very unknown.

☐ I struggle with shame and feelings of inadequacy.

Parts of myself I don't share with the world as a Four:

☐ I doubt myself often.

☐ I am very sensitive to other people's reactions toward me.

☐ I constantly compare myself to the version of me I have made up in my mind.

☐ I have a hard time seeing the gifts and talents within myself.

☐ I have a hard time seeing the value I bring into the world.

☐ I struggle with social anxiety.

Parts of myself I don't share with the world as a Five:

☐ I fear my needs are too intense for others to handle.

☐ I'm afraid that I will be rejected if I seek warmth and connection.

☐ I do not like to need others for fear of losing my autonomy.

☐ I fear looking foolish or incompetent.

☐ I desire to find someone who is safe and comforting.

☐ If I feel my autonomy is at risk, I may leave the relationship.

Parts of myself I don't share with the world as a Six:

☐ I want things to be in order to keep inner peace.

☐ Predictable patterns make me feel safe.

☐ My internal thoughts cause me to second-guess myself.

☐ I have a hard time making decisions because of the constant chatter in my mind.

☐ I really need inner peace, but instead I often busy myself as a way of distracting the noise.

☐ Fear often keeps me from living up to my full potential.

☐ Even though I am very loyal, I am afraid of trusting the wrong person.

☐ I don't like to attempt new things if I'm not sure I will succeed.

Parts of myself I don't share with the world as a Seven:

☐ I struggle with feelings of anxiety, sadness, and anger.

☐ I seek adventure to escape overwhelming feelings.

☐ I struggle with self-doubt.

☐ I am fearful of being abandoned or rejected if I show my true emotions.

☐ I fear I will always feel a deep emptiness within.

☐ I avoid unpleasant feelings by being upbeat and happy.

Parts of myself I don't share with the world as an Eight:

- ☐ I actually have a very tender heart but I fear being vulnerable.
- ☐ I take control of situations because I do not like being seen as incompetent or unnecessary.
- ☐ I don't trust people easily, so I am always on guard.
- ☐ I long to know someone is looking out for me.
- ☐ I feel I must portray a strong, confident demeanor at all times.
- ☐ I do not respect those who are lazy or incompetent.

Parts of myself I don't share with the world as a Nine:

- ☐ I struggle with feelings of anger and sometimes rage under the surface.
- ☐ I do not always enjoy going with the flow.
- ☐ I desire to have autonomy and independence.
- ☐ I would love not to be bothered by life or people.
- ☐ I will attempt to keep peace so my inner world stays calm.
- ☐ Even though I don't share them often, I have very strong thoughts and opinions.
- ☐ I want people to think of my needs sometimes.

In the activity for this section, notice that I've added a circle at the top called the "marriage circle." In this circle, you and your partner will begin to unpack the ways you both desire to be loved and cared for. Over the next several weeks you will continue to add to this circle, and by the end of this workbook you will discover you've written a new rhythm for the way you want to love, care for, honor, and respect one another.

Activity

Start by each of you writing your Enneagram type on the line above your circle. Inside your circle write the core fears for your type that you most relate to. Now, each of you write a sentence in the marriage circle that will help your partner understand what you need from them to combat your fears. For example, "I fear being rejected, so when I'm talking to you it's helpful if you turn your attention to me and make eye contact." The more you are each willing to express your vulnerabilities, the more emotionally connected you will become.

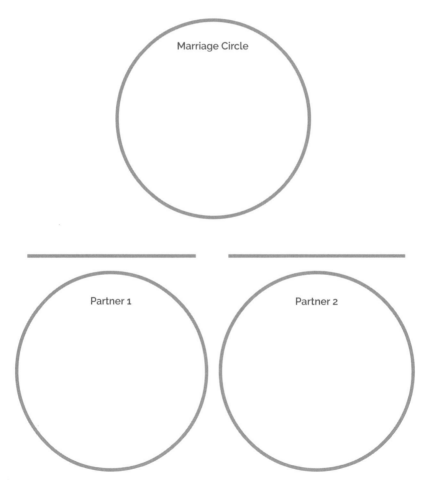

Marriage Circle

Partner 1

Partner 2

Questions

In conflict with your partner, which response do you most often use?

Partner 1:

Partner 2:

How have you witnessed your core fears being activated and causing conflict within your relationships?

Partner 1:

Partner 2:

What are a few things you have learned about your partner through awareness of their core fears?

Partner 1:

Partner 2:

What do you need from your partner to feel safe and secure in your relationship?

Partner 1:

Partner 2:

WEEK 3

Growing Together through Communication and Connection

Heart Longing Messages and Core Desires

Your task is not to seek for love, but merely to seek and find all the barriers within yourself that you have built against it.

Rumi

Communication and connection are the building blocks of a healthy, thriving relationship. Learning how to communicate with your partner allows for clear understanding and spoken expectations. The better you learn how to communicate with each other, the better you will understand and connect with each other. Connection is not just a physical act but also an emotional one. Learning what matters to your partner and what they need to hear will bring you closer together.

The bond you create through communication and connection will help build trust. The more intentionality you put toward understanding your partner, the stronger your foundation will be as life unfolds. You might be great at communication and connection, or you might struggle. Either way, by learning about the heart longing messages for your Enneagram types, you will have words to speak to one another that help you feel loved and cared for. Going a step further and diving in to your type's core desires will enable you to love one another with a better understanding of what each of you is looking for in life.

Your heart longing message is a message you needed to hear from your parents in childhood. You may have heard this message at times, but perhaps not as often as you needed in order to feel safe, seen, and secure.

Maybe you've never really thought about what motivates your patterns of behavior. But as you become aware of your heart longing message, you will also become aware of what it is you really desire. You will be able to unpack the ways your ego-self has been directing your steps as you try to protect yourself and get your needs met. Riso and Hudson believe our "ego agenda" is what drives our patterns of behavior.[1] The ego can be explained as "the only part of the conscious personality. It's what the person is aware of when they think about themselves, and is what they usually try to project toward others."[2]

Because your ego-self is focused on protecting your heart longing message and is the driving force behind your desires, you might find that you have been stuck in a cycle of behavior that is no longer serving you. You might find that your drive to protect your heart longing and your push to get your needs met often cause you to keep chasing after the same thing by using the same strategies and hoping for a different outcome, leaving you disappointed, discouraged, and disconnected.

Humans often repeat familiar patterns of behavior in trying to get their needs met, and these patterns stem from early childhood. According to social worker Sharon Martin, "We repeat what we learned as children. The beliefs, coping skills, and behavior patterns that we learned in childhood become deeply entrenched because we learned them when we were vulnerable, and our brains weren't fully developed. And after years of using them, they are hard to change."[3] As you can imagine, the need to protect ourselves and the desire to get our needs met can cause major communication issues within our relationships.

If you don't feel safe and seen within your marriage, it is unlikely that you will lower your protective armor and let your partner see your vulnerable side. If you don't feel secure within the relationship, you will continue to function from your ego-self, protecting your heart longing message and your core desires for fear of rejection, abandonment, or neglect. However, if you allow yourself to see your heart longing message through a new lens and begin to acknowledge the ways you have tried to get your core desires met, you will begin to unlock the key to beautiful connection and heart-based communication.

As you and your partner explore this week's topics on heart longing messages and core desires, be mindful of each other and the vulnerability that is being exposed. Make it a point to listen to your partner with an open mind and try to understand where they are coming from. Be aware of your attempts to fix them or to reframe the words that they share with you. This awareness is a very tender part of each of your stories, and it's one of the foundational messages that has been at work in your lives, creating patterns of behavior in hopes of getting your needs met. It is also important to mention that your heart longing message and your core desires represent basic human needs, so understand that there is nothing wrong with expressing your needs and desires.

Uncovering Your Heart Longing Message

Sarah and Ben had been dating for over two years. They cared deeply for one another, but the thought of spending the rest of their lives together made them feel anxious and overwhelmed. They felt pressure from family and friends who were always talking about the future and asking when they could expect a wedding invitation.

Sarah is a One and Ben is a Six. They are loyal and committed to each other, so that is not the hang-up. Their hesitation is based in their heart longings. Before they learned their Enneagram numbers and started to really dive into understanding each other through this new lens, they often felt nervous about expressing their feelings. Sarah found herself second-guessing what Ben said and constantly looked for signs of what he "really thought" of her. She even found herself retreating from the relationship if she could not decipher the meaning of a look he gave her. Sarah felt so conflicted. She loved and trusted Ben, but she still had a deeply rooted fear that he would not see her as good and that he would reject or abandon her at some point.

Ben was head over heels in love with Sarah, but he often felt confused and nervous because he couldn't quite read her. His attempts to compliment her or to share his feelings would often be met with a disconnected response. He found himself asking her questions he already knew the answers to just to see if she would tell him the truth. Her retreating and withdrawing caused Ben so much anxiety that he sometimes felt like calling it quits, which made him feel defensive. But at the end of the day, he really believed they were right for each other, so he continued to pursue Sarah in hopes that one day she would believe his intentions were true.

Once they began to dig into their personalities using the helpful tool of the Enneagram, they began to see the root causes of their anxiety and overwhelming feelings. Ben had been trying to love Sarah through his own heart longing message of "You are safe," but that is not what she needed. Ben finally understood that Sarah needed to hear the words "You are good" and know that he would be supportive, kind, and compassionate if she made a mistake. Sarah, on the other hand, started to understand that her desire to protect herself by withdrawing and retreating from the relationship whenever she felt scared or triggered was the very issue that was causing Ben to become anxious and irritable. Ben's heart longing message is to know he is safe, so when Sarah pulled away emotionally or physically from the relationship, it left Ben feeling scared.

Today, Sarah and Ben understand the importance of asking clarifying questions and giving each other the benefit of the doubt. They are finally planning a wedding and, more importantly, a dream life together. They have chosen to focus on investing their time, energy, and efforts into understanding each other and allowing each other the space to be who they are. They champion and at times challenge one another to become better in all areas of their lives.

. . . . . .

You and your partner each have a specific message that your heart has longed to hear since childhood, a message that Riso and Hudson refer to as your "lost childhood message."[4] This heart longing message was not received in the way you needed it as a child and therefore has been another motivating factor in the development of your behavior patterns. Over the years you have learned to adapt those patterns in hopes of receiving what you needed from your parents, loved ones, role models, and even your spouse.

Your heart longing message is very much active in your life today. You still long to have this message met through words, actions, and deeds. You most likely seek people and situations that will help fulfill this message, or perhaps you've built walls around this message so your heart doesn't get hurt. It may be difficult for you to look back and explore where this heart longing came from; however, when you are able to acknowledge parts of yourself and your history so you can begin to change familiar behavior patterns that no longer serve you, the important work of understanding, self-awareness, and healing occurs.

This is a hard truth but one you must understand: *you have to feel to heal*. So allow yourself to reflect, acknowledge, and feel as you read the heart longing message for each Enneagram type in the image below. Be mindful

The Message You Long to Hear

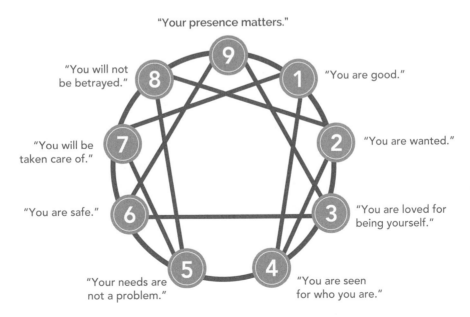

"Your presence matters."

"You will not be betrayed."

"You are good."

"You are wanted."

"You will be taken care of."

"You are safe."

"You are loved for being yourself."

"Your needs are not a problem."

"You are seen for who you are."

of how your heart longing message has affected your marriage relationship in the past and may still be affecting it today.

Now to bring you hope! This longing message does not mean you are a lost cause or destined for relational failure—quite the contrary, actually. As you begin to unpack your heart longing message, you become more aware of what you need and how to effectively ask for it within your marriage. With this new awareness about your partner, you also have the opportunity to choose to intentionally care for them in a way that speaks to their heart longing message. This type of loving care and concern is what helps sustain emotional connections within relationships.

Here are a few suggestions as you and your partner learn to love and nurture each other's heart longing message. Find your partner's number below and make it a point to start putting these strategies into practice.

Ones

Actively listen so you understand what their expectation is.

Be honest.

Own your mistakes.

Understand they can be a little over-the-top with perfectionism, but it really matters to them.

Tell them what positive attributes you see in them.

Twos

Tell them often that you are thinking about them and they matter to you.

Don't rush them; they need time to process what they need.

They enjoy being around people who are upbeat and positive, so be mindful of negativity.

Make it a point to tell them what they are doing is making a difference and matters.

Be careful how you correct them, as they care deeply about what other people think.

Threes

Do what you say you're going to do.

Allow them to get stuff done with little interruption.

Engage them in their fast-paced plans.

Plan ahead for time together.

Praise and acknowledge them for their hard work, even if they shy away from it.

Fours

Try to understand where they are coming from.

Allow them to express themselves without trying to fix them.

Let them know that you value them and their unique perspective.

Be authentic and allow them to be their true self.

Take time to connect with them in a way that conveys you know, understand, and value them, such as playing their favorite music, going to an art museum, or engaging in a conversation about what interests them.

Fives

Understand that their need for privacy has nothing to do with you.

Stick to the timelines that you lay out.

Clearly tell them what your expectations are.

Respect their need for space.

Always give them a heads-up, as they don't really like surprises.

Sixes

Be honest, open, and clear about what you think and want.

Be patient with them as they ask questions.

Try to understand their fears and worries, and don't judge them for being fearful or anxious.

Value their ability to assess risks and troubleshoot.

Help them to take action on things they want to do.

Sevens

Plan upbeat, positive activities to do together.

Allow them to express themselves without criticism.

Allow them the freedom and flexibility to get stuff done in their own way.

Support and encourage them to think through the possibilities that are in front of them.

Think about them and include them when making decisions.

Eights

Tell them the truth and don't hide things from them.

Affirm the gifts you see within them.

Get behind them when they take action.

Don't undermine their authority; instead, offer support.

Spend time listening to their ideas and allow them to dream.

Nines

Make an effort and pay attention to what they are interested in.

Be gentle and kind to them as they process what you are asking them.

Let them know you value others' opinions as well as theirs.

Be understanding of their sensitivity to conflict and criticism.

Make it a point to ask them what they think or want.

The activity below is meant to help you pause and process this tender part of yourself, so find a quiet spot and sit with this information for a little while before you start.

 *Activity*

Once you are ready, each of you will write your heart longing message on the line above your circle. Inside your circle, write the ways you have tried to get your heart longing met, or perhaps the ways you have protected that longing in your relationship. Then, in the marriage circle, each of you will write one sentence that will help your partner understand what you need from them to help build trust and connection within your relationship. An example might be, "I am fearful of being rejected, so it's helpful when you turn your attention to me and make eye contact when I'm talking to you." The more each of you is willing to express your vulnerabilities with the other, the more emotionally connected you will become.

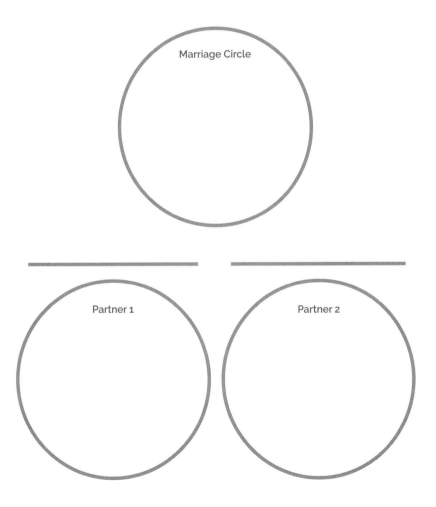

▨▨▨ *Questions* ▨▨▨

As you review your Enneagram number's heart longing message, what are some of the ways it has shaped who you are today?

Partner 1:

Partner 2:

Recount a time from your childhood when you felt like your heart longing message was fulfilled.

Partner 1:

Partner 2:

What patterns of behavior do you think stem from your heart longing message?

Partner 1:

Partner 2:

How have those patterns caused conflict within your relationship?

Partner 1:

Partner 2:

How can you show compassion toward your partner as they explore their own heart longing message?

Partner 1:

Partner 2:

In what ways can you support each other as you both become more aware of how your heart longing message is impacting your day-to-day life and relationship?

Partner 1:

Partner 2:

In what ways can you show your partner love and compassion by affirming their heart longing message with what they need to hear and know about themselves today?

Partner 1:

Partner 2:

────────── **Identifying Core Desires** ──────────

Michael and Nicki have been dating for a little over three years. Michael is ready to take the next step and propose, but Nicki is very hesitant. They have taken their time getting to know each other while also learning more about themselves. Nicki does not want to repeat the mistakes her parents made, so she wants to be certain this is the right next step.

Nicki is an Enneagram Six and is concerned with safety and security. She likes to investigate and research everything before she makes decisions. She wishes there were a way she could know that she and Michael are going to make it "till death do us part." Nicki believes that her parents rushed into marriage; after all, they got married after dating just over a year, claiming they were young and in love. They were married for fifteen years when her mother came home one day and said she'd had enough. She no longer loved her husband and she no longer wanted to be married. This news shocked Nicki's father. He had missed the signals that something was wrong and thought they were happy. Because of that experience, Nicki has had a hard time trusting that Michael won't decide to walk out on her and their children. What Nicki needs to know is that Michael is choosing her and that she is safe with him. She also needs to know that Michael understands just how big of an issue this is for her and that his reassurance is not a suggestion but rather a need and desire.

Michael, on the other hand, is a Nine. He was raised by parents who were honest about the hard seasons and chose to fight for their marriage even when it was hard. Michael's parents have actively sought counseling throughout their marriage to help them process difficult seasons and to help them stay connected and grow toward each other. Michael understands the reality of life after marriage and knows without a shadow of a doubt that Nicki is the love of his life. Michael really desires to be at peace in his life and in his relationship with Nicki, and he believes he knows what that will require. He is willing to work at creating a home filled with peace and predictability so that Nicki knows she is safe. He, in turn, wants Nicki to help create an environment that is harmonious and peaceful, not critical, suspicious, or nitpicking.

As Nicki and Michael have learned more about themselves through Enneagram awareness, they have been able to have open and honest conversations about what they want, need, and desire from one another. They also have been able to proactively give love and support to one another from a place of understanding, not resentment or frustration. Michael and Nicki are ready to get engaged and take the next step into their future together with loving support and kindness.

· · · · · ·

This week you have been working on building a solid foundation in your relationship through healthy communication and understanding. One of the strengths of the Enneagram system is how it reveals deeply rooted motivations and inner messages for each type. In this section you are going to explore your core desires. The core desires for each type are closely tied to its heart longing message. These foundational elements will allow you and your partner to put words to your greatest longing, which will lead to some vulnerable conversations. But if you both participate in this exercise of vulnerability, you will build a strong connection that consists of security, trust, and love.

The idea of *core desires* refers to what each Enneagram type longs for and strives to gain in order to live a fulfilling life. These patterns are established at a young age. To have your core desires met means you feel fully seen and fully known. To feel fully seen and fully known takes time, patience, and connection. When you fully see and fully know your partner, you allow them to be their authentic self. You don't expect them to show up as the person you would like them to be, and you don't filter who they are through your own fears and desires. Instead, you embrace them for who they are and celebrate their uniqueness, creativity, passions, gifts, talents, thoughts, and ideas as they continue to grow into the fullness of who they have been created to be. Empathy and compassion enable each of you to see the other through a lens of curiosity and kindness instead of judgment and defensiveness. People want to be heard, not fixed, and seen, not silenced.

Below are descriptions of core desires for each Enneagram type. Take a few minutes and consider the core desires for your number. Allow yourself to acknowledge which statements are true for you, and check the boxes accordingly.

Ones desire to be fair, thorough, and objective.

☐ I want to be seen as a person of integrity.

☐ I want to live a balanced life.

☐ I seek justice and truthfulness.

☐ I want to do what is ethical and right.

☐ I want my partner to see me as a good person.

Twos desire to be cared for, loved, and wanted.

☐ I want to be in an emotionally connected and loving relationship.

☐ I want to be celebrated, not tolerated.

☐ I want to know my partner will not overlook my needs.

☐ I want to know I am valued within our relationship.

Threes desire to be seen as valuable and worthy of love.

☐ I want to receive affirmation.

☐ I want to be seen as valuable.

☐ I want to simply be myself without having to perform.

☐ I want to find rest and contentment with my partner.

Fours desire to be authentic and accepted as their unique self.

☐ I want my partner to validate the unique significance I bring to the world.

☐ I want to be accepted just as I am.

☐ I want to be understood.

☐ I want my partner to love me even when I am expressing my big emotions.

☐ I want to hear life-giving affirmation.

Fives desire to be knowledgeable and competent.

☐ I want to be seen as capable and competent.

☐ I want my partner to help me feel safe and comfortable.

☐ I want to be understood.

☐ I want a partner who will meet my needs.

☐ I gather knowledge as a way of feeling safe in the world.

Sixes desire to be safe and secure.

☐ I want to have a partner who offers guidance and support.

☐ I want to feel security and connection.

☐ I want to have a safe environment where our relationship can flourish.

☐ I want to feel supported and have healthy communication.

☐ I want to feel listened to and understood.

Sevens desire to be fulfilled and content.

☐ I want to be in a happy and joyful relationship.

☐ I want to experience excitement and satisfaction.

☐ I want to find fulfillment in life.

☐ I want to be in a relationship where I feel safe to express my emotions.

☐ I want to know I am loved and cared for.

Eights desire to be self-sufficient and strong.

☐ I want to protect myself and those I love.

☐ I want my partner to see me as smart, competent, and strong.

☐ I want to be respected and validated.

☐ I want my partner to support me as I make a big difference in the world.

☐ I want to be the best version of myself.

Nines desire to have serenity and live in harmony.

☐ I want inner stability and peace of mind.

☐ I want to avoid conflict and chaos within relationships.

☐ I want to live in a harmonious environment.

☐ I want my partner to make me feel seen and show me that my presence matters.

☐ I want to be loved and appreciated.

Each Enneagram type needs to know certain truths as they seek to overcome their core fear and gain their core desire through emotional connection within their marriage relationship.

Ones: You are loved and valued even if you make a mistake.

Twos: You are loved even when you express your own needs and desires.

Threes: You are loved even when you share your true thoughts, feelings, and ideas.

Fours: You are loved even when your emotions are all over the place and larger than life.

Fives: You are loved even when you retreat into your own space and thoughts.

Sixes: You are loved and supported as you pursue your passion, even in the face of fear.

Sevens: You are loved and cared for even when you panic and feel trapped.

Eights: You are loved and cared for even when you let your guard down and show your more vulnerable side.

Nines: You are loved even when you speak up and share your thoughts.

To help you process and express your core desires, it is important that you engage in the activity below. When you engage in a writing activity that allows you to explore your deeper thoughts and feelings, it enables the words to come to life. As you write down your core desires, you will more likely be able to acknowledge your needs. Growth for each of you in this area means remaining open to your partner and their willingness to respond to your needs. You are encouraged to explore the ways acknowledging these desires will strengthen your relationship.

Activity

Each of you write your Enneagram number on the line above your circle and write your core desires inside your circle. In the marriage circle each of you write one sentence starting with "I see your core desires and I promise I will _____ to help honor you and those desires."

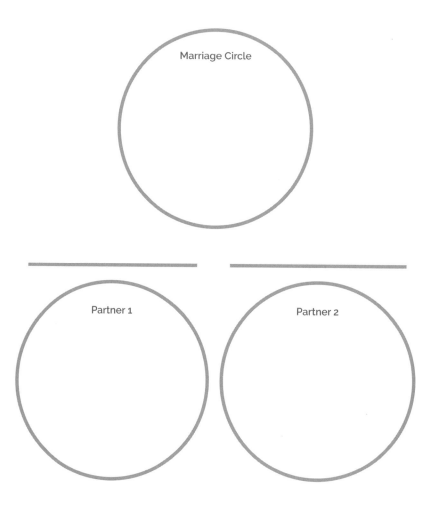

Questions

As you read the core desires for your Enneagram type, what thoughts or feelings began to surface for you?

Partner 1:

Partner 2:

In what ways have you protected and defended your core desires?

Partner 1:

Partner 2:

List three practical ways you would like your partner to care for you in regard to your core desires.

Partner 1:

1. _____

2. _____

3. _____

Partner 2:

1. _____

2. _____

3. _____

In what ways has reading about your partner's core desires helped you understand them better?

Partner 1:

Partner 2:

What do you think would happen if you and your partner made a concerted effort to nurture each other's core desires?

Partner 1:

Partner 2:

WEEK 4

Leveling Up

Triads and Stances

We have to dare to be ourselves however frightening or strange that self may prove to be.

May Sarton

Understanding and accepting yourself is essential to your ability to love and connect with your partner. A healthy relationship is both autonomous and connected. That might seem confusing. How are you supposed to be independent as well as joined? Well, in a healthy relationship you are not looking for someone else to complete you. Instead, you are looking for someone who will come alongside you with support, love, kindness, and faithfulness. Someone who champions you to do the things you are passionate about and gives you the freedom to be authentically you. Figuring out your authentic self requires curiosity, exploration, and openness. And in order to love your partner well you also have to allow them to be authentically who they are.

This week we will explore Enneagram triads and stances, which offer insight into the ways we process information, try to get our needs met, and try to solve inner conflict. These two pieces of Enneagram awareness will open your eyes to how you have attempted to protect yourself by suppressing parts of yourself. They will also give insight into the ways you have limited yourself without even realizing it.

We'll begin by exploring Enneagram *triads*, which many great Enneagram teachers refer to as the "centers of intelligence."[1] The centers of intelligence make up the three basic building blocks of the human psyche: Heart (feelings), Head (thoughts), and Gut (instincts). Regardless of which triad a person is in, we each possess all three components; however, one of them is typically blocked or distorted. Not until we do the work to uncover the one that is blocked and figure out why it is blocked or distorted will we have access to all three. When one of the triads is blocked or distorted, it causes us to build defensive walls as we try to protect ourselves from possible dangers. Understanding the triads is useful for knowing how we process information and deal with our emotions. Each triad exposes an imbalance in the ways we either overuse or underuse our Heart, Head, and Gut.

We'll then explore Enneagram *stances*, which were first developed by psychologist Karen Horney. She wrote about how people try to get their needs met in one of three distinct ways: by being compliant, expansive, or detached (or compliant, assertive, or withdrawn) from others as they try to process information and keep themselves safe. Kathy Hurley and Theodore Dobson then expanded on Horney's ideas to show how our stance is essential to the way we communicate within our relationships. Enneagram stances make us aware of the ways we unconsciously pursue our desires. Learning about your stance and your partner's stance will greatly benefit your understanding of situations and your ability to communicate with one another. You will finally have insight into your partner's protective layer, and this will allow for vulnerability and build trust. This awareness will help you as a couple to feel safe and secure in your relationship so you can function autonomously while at the same time leaning into connection.

Exploring the Triads

Roxanne and Dillan have been dating for a little over a year, and they really desire to take their relationship to the next level. They are both passionate about fitness and living a healthy lifestyle. They enjoy the same activities, love to try new restaurants, and share the same taste in music. All of this seems like it would make for an easy relationship, yet they keep coming up against the same issue. Roxanne, a Four, feels things deeply; her mood and motivation can be greatly affected by her environment. Dillan, an Eight, moves through life with passion and force. He experiences life by going after what he desires and making things happen.

This, at times, leaves Roxanne feeling overwhelmed or even overlooked. She likes to take her time and process how she feels or thinks about the experiences they enjoy, such as tasting a new dish on the menu or seeing a new band in concert. Dillan, on the other hand, prefers to enjoy their experiences and move on to the next thing rather quickly. He doesn't like to sit in his feelings, so he struggles to have patience with Roxanne when she tries prompting him to be more open and vulnerable about what he is thinking and feeling.

Once Dillan and Roxanne began taking a deeper dive into their personality types through the lens of the Enneagram, they started to understand each other better. As a Four, Roxanne is in the Heart Triad. She is in tune with her feelings and often gets caught up in her emotions, to the point where she is unable to see the bigger picture. She wants Dillan to mirror her emotions and concern back to her so she feels seen and supported. As an Eight, however, Dillan is in the Gut Triad. He is decisive and moves according to what feels right. He has good instincts and doesn't like to waste a lot of time on the what-ifs of life. He also wants Roxanne to mirror his excitement, concern, and even frustration to help him feel more grounded and understood. As they have learned to have patience with each other and to try seeing things from the other person's perspective, they have found a new love and connection.

· · · · · ·

Do you find yourself feeling misunderstood or confused by your partner's responses? Have you ever walked away from a conversation feeling frustrated and bothered because your partner did not see the situation the same way you did? Such feelings are common when you each function from a different triad. The Enneagram triads correspond to the three centers of intelligence: head, heart, and gut. The three Enneagram types within each triad share common traits, views, and vices that inform their behavioral patterns. Everyone has access to all three centers of intelligence; however, people tend to draw largely from only one.

**Head or
Thinking Triad**
Enneagram numbers
5, 6, 7

**Heart or
Feelings Triad**
Enneagram numbers
2, 3, 4

**Instinctual or
Gut Triad**
Enneagram numbers
8, 9, 1

The Heart Triad

The Heart Triad focuses on finding value and love. However, those in this triad are fearful of letting their guard down and allowing others to see them as they are. In their book *The Wisdom of the Enneagram*, Riso and Hudson write, "At the deepest level, your heart qualities are the source of your identity. When your heart opens, you know who you are, and that 'who you are' has nothing to do with what people think of you and nothing to do with your past history."[2] At their core, individuals in the Heart Triad know this to be true, but they often don't know how to live free from other people's opinions of them. They therefore work hard to develop an appealing self-image and will often trade deep emotional connection for surface affection and affirmation.

Twos, Threes, and Fours make up the Heart Triad. This means they overprocess or underprocess information primarily through their feelings. This triad desires attention, but because they don't want to appear needy, they struggle with allowing others to know the depth of how they feel. They don't want to put themselves in a position where their heart can get hurt, so they use their strengths to protect themselves by building a self-image that others find appealing and likable. They tend to seek affirmation and acceptance by looking to others to see what is acceptable and appropriate. Because of this, those in the Heart Triad often struggle with finding their true identity.

The Heart Triad deals with underlying issues of shame, which Brené Brown defines as "the intensely painful feeling or experience of believing that we are flawed and therefore unworthy of love, belonging, and connection."[3] Shame causes you to tell yourself "I am the bad thing I did," and because of that you retreat and withdraw from others. As a result, those in the Heart Triad try to keep others at arm's length, which then moves them away from relational connection.

Here are specific characteristics for each Enneagram type within the Heart Triad. Check the boxes that you resonate with as a Two, Three, or Four.

Twos

☐ They work hard to be seen as acceptable, kind, caring people who are willing to help and serve others as a way to avoid feelings of shame.

☐ They try to earn attention by serving and doing thoughtful things for others.

☐ They are naturally affectionate, supportive, helpful people who display generosity and compassion.

☐ To avoid feelings of shame, they seek validation by becoming indispensable to their loved ones.

☐ To avoid being rejected, they suppress feelings of anger, frustration, and self-indulgence, and can convince themselves they don't have needs in an effort to be low maintenance.

Threes

☐ They put their energy and attention toward achieving and performing as a way of being seen as successful so they can combat feelings of shame.

- [ ] They demand attention by doing whatever wins them recognition and admiration.
- [ ] They focus on improving themselves and are great motivators.
- [ ] They adapt their self-image to what is valued in any situation.
- [ ] They tend to suppress their emotions and lose touch with their personal feelings to avoid shame.
- [ ] They seek affirmation and acceptance but can lose touch with their core self while trying to earn it.
- [ ] They try to dodge shame by highlighting their achievements.

Fours

- [ ] They avoid feelings of shame by overprocessing and dismissing the role they played in a difficult or hurtful situation and oftentimes by viewing themselves as the victim in the situation.
- [ ] They withdraw for attention in hopes that someone will see them as worth pursuing.
- [ ] They are authentic and self-revealing.
- [ ] They maintain an image of being unique to combat the shame that their lives are not meaningful.
- [ ] As an expressive type, they encourage others to process their emotions because they believe it is better to deal with emotions than to suppress them.
- [ ] They tend to feel melancholy and misunderstood, and at times they are prone to struggling with depression, isolation, and shame.

The Head Triad

The Head Triad focuses on "finding a sense of inner guidance and support."[4] This triad struggles with a strong desire for safety and security. They naturally process how a situation will impact them and their environment, and at times this complicates how they respond because either they overthink and overplan or they abandon all thoughts just to protect themselves. They have a hard time quieting their mind and being fully present in the moment.

Their mind goes a mile a minute, and they are constantly thinking through new ideas, scenarios, and possibilities.

Enneagram Fives, Sixes, and Sevens are in the Head Triad. This means that they make decisions and react to the world by compiling and processing information. Each type tries to make sense of their feelings by accumulating and applying knowledge in a way that fits with their number's common behaviors. The inability to quiet their mind can cause nervous energy and distrust within themselves as they try to make decisions that will impact their life. They seek to find security through gathering knowledge; however, underlying feelings of fear keep them from truly letting their guard down and trusting people, institutions, and authority.

The Head Triad deals with underlying issues of anxiety. The American Psychological Association describes anxiety as "feelings of tension, worried thoughts, and physical changes like increased blood pressure."[5] In her book *Atlas of the Heart*, Brené Brown suggests that anxiety often leads to one of two coping strategies: worry or avoidance. Worry causes you to get caught up in thinking about negative thoughts regarding possible future issues, and avoidance causes you to withdraw and retreat from others, which moves you away from the connection into isolation. Individuals in the Head Triad attempt to stave off their feelings of anxiety by seeking inner guidance, keeping themselves constantly busy and on the go, or seeking outside support people or resources.

Here are specific characteristics for each Enneagram type within the Head Triad. Check the boxes that you resonate with as a Five, Six, or Seven.

Fives

☐ They believe that others are not dependable when it comes to support and guidance, so to quiet their inner fears and anxieties they take it upon themselves to gather the resources they need so they don't have to rely on anyone else.

☐ They withdraw for security, thinking they will be safe if they gather everything they need and do not have to look outside themselves for support.

☐ They are deep thinkers who have a thirst for knowledge.

☐ They invent new ideas, strategies, concepts, and items based on the things they learn.

☐ They fear failure, so they gather knowledge to feel secure and use that information to combat feelings of anxiety.

☐ They tend to feel easily overwhelmed by the world and prefer to interact from a detached state.

Sixes

☐ They try to quiet their fears and anxieties by seeking guidance and support from a strong, competent, trustworthy individual who can teach them to be independent and self-sufficient, although they often become dependent on this person.

☐ Sixes try to earn security by being prepared and doing what they believe is expected of them.

☐ They are systematic thinkers and excellent problem solvers.

☐ They value loyalty and deep friendship.

☐ They fear making the wrong decision, so they look for outside support and guidance to calm their anxiety.

☐ They can also be suspicious and fearful of untested authority.

☐ Planners by nature, they think through situations in great detail. Because of this, they can get caught up in imagining worst-case scenarios, which can amplify their extreme anxiety and worry.

Sevens

☐ They try to conquer their fears and anxieties by keeping themselves in situations and relationships that allow them to be independent and free to make their own choices.

☐ They demand security by going after whatever they feel will make them feel safe and secure.

☐ They are quick-minded and excellent multitaskers, but they over-extend themselves by taking on too many tasks.

☐ They seek pleasure to distract themselves from feelings of insecurity, and they become restless when they are stressed.

☐ They will do anything to avoid feeling sad, lonely, and depressed—emotions that cause them anxiety—which can make them seem shallow and flighty.

☐ They are future-oriented, fear loss and abandonment, and live for new experiences.

The Gut Triad

Those who are in the Gut Triad focus on protecting themselves from outside influences that could in any way affect them, their environment, or their life. Riso and Hudson describe this triad as "attempting to use their will to affect the world without being affected by it."[6] Individuals in this triad struggle with anger and rage that stem from childhood, when at times they felt they had to suppress their emotions in an attempt to make themselves small and unseen. Because of this, they seek autonomy by not letting others get too close, keeping parts of their life separate, and even keeping secrets from their loved ones.

Enneagram Eights, Nines, and Ones are in the Gut Triad. They overuse or underuse their intuition to process information and make decisions. They often have a physical reaction to information and situations that helps them assess what they are experiencing. They have a strong "knowing" within themselves, which causes them to either move forward into situations with force or move away from them for the sake of safety. They seek to maintain control over their personal lives and environments as a way to keep themselves steady and unaffected by their surroundings. While they tend to crave justice and peace, these types are also prone to feelings of resentment when others do not think and act in ways that match up with their worldview.

Those in the Gut Triad struggle with aggression, passive aggression, and repression. Brené Brown describes anger as "an emotion that we feel when something gets in the way of the desired outcome or when we believe there's a violation of the way things should be done."[7] The anger felt by those in the Gut Triad can cause mental and physical health issues when left unresolved. It has a way of masking deeper emotions, such as sadness, loneliness, overwhelm, and betrayal. If used as an excuse to withdraw or explode, it can also cause disconnection, fear, and confusion within a person's relationships.

Here are specific characteristics for each Enneagram type within the Gut Triad. Check the boxes that you resonate with as an Eight, Nine, or One.

Eights

- ☐ They tend to express themselves boldly and act out their feelings of anger or rage.
- ☐ They demand autonomy and the ability to have freedom and independence.
- ☐ They are perceptive and in tune to what is happening in their environment.
- ☐ They repress their fears and vulnerabilities and often fight for the underdog.
- ☐ They desire to control their environment because they don't want to be controlled by others.
- ☐ They fear being betrayed and can react in aggressive ways out of anger.

Nines

- ☐ They tend to suppress their anger and rage, knowing that these feelings bubble just below the surface yet unwilling to allow them to rise until everything comes to a head and they explode.
- ☐ They withdraw to gain autonomy and seek inner harmony.
- ☐ Receptive and open-minded, they are naturally attuned to what other people are feeling and will compromise to avoid feelings of anger or discomfort.
- ☐ They are prone to giving up their own identities for the sake of harmony.

☐ They are acutely aware of how other people are being perceived and desire to create environments where others can grow and flourish.

☐ Unnerved by their underlying anger, they attempt to control their thoughts and suppress their feelings in an effort to escape potential conflict.

Ones

☐ They tend to repress their feelings of anger and rage, acting as if those feelings don't exist, so that they don't appear to others as bad or corrupt.

☐ They attempt to earn autonomy by being good or perfect so that their inner world is not disturbed and they are able to control their outward expression.

☐ They are wise, levelheaded, fair-minded people who are guided by their principles.

☐ They possess a strong sense of self-knowledge and work hard to keep themselves in line.

☐ They repress and deny the parts of themselves that don't conform to what they believe is acceptable.

☐ Often grieved by things they believe are unjust or unfair, they can become resentful when others do not agree with them.

☐ They seek to create order as a way of establishing peace in their lives.

Understanding and accepting yourself is the first step in processing your Enneagram triad. In the activity below, take some time this week to process your triad and gain greater self-awareness and acceptance. Once you and your partner have each spent time alone processing your triads, complete the final part of the activity together.

Activity

Today's activity is a prompt to simply write down your thoughts and feelings about the information you have read in this section. Writing down the new awareness you have gained about your Enneagram triad will help you understand your thoughts and feelings more clearly. Triad awareness often takes time to process. Give yourself grace as you identify how your triad has been actively trying to protect you as you engage the world around you.

The Heart Triad

Find a quiet place within your home or in nature. Put your hand on your heart and take a deep breath in for a count of four, then slowly release your breath for a count of four. Do this two more times or until you feel settled and relaxed. Next, notice your heart. What sensations are you feeling as you allow your thoughts to drift toward your heart? Does your heart feel full, warm, sharp, or perhaps achy? What color would you give your heart? Now cup your hands together and visualize holding what your heart feels like and the color that you pictured. As you hold space for these feelings to exist, speak a few sentences to your heart that you believe will bring comfort and love. For example, "I see you, heart. I see you shattered and tattered, and I see the color yellow over these feelings. The yellow I see is a ray of hope and warmth. I am going to care for you and pay attention to what you need."

The Head Triad

Go outside and stand in the grass. With your eyes open and your hands resting on your chest, take two deep breaths in and out. Notice where you are and name it. ("I am in my backyard.") Notice what you are seeing around you. ("I see a bluebird, clouds in the sky, and green grass.") Notice the temperature outside. ("The sun is warm on my face.") What thoughts are surfacing? What stress and anxiety can you release as you breathe in and out, staying present with your body? Allow the thoughts to surface, and as they do, hold them for a minute and acknowledge them, then blow them away from you like a bubble. Repeat this until you feel relaxed and peaceful.

The Gut Triad

Find a quiet and comfortable place to sit on the floor. Close your eyes and take a deep breath in and out. Do this two more times. Now think about a body part that feels tense. Allow your mind to register what is causing the tension, then take a deep breath in. As you breathe out, let the tension you are feeling in that body part be released. Continue to do this with every part of your body where you are feeling the tension. When you finish, stand up and slowly extend your hands above your head as you take a deep breath in, then lower your hands as you exhale.

Write your Enneagram triad on the line above your circle. Next, circle the word—attention, security, or autonomy—that aligns with your Enneagram triad. Inside your circle write the ways you have tried to achieve attention, security, or autonomy according to your triad. For example, "I pay attention to what people are interested in so I know what topics to bring up in conversation."

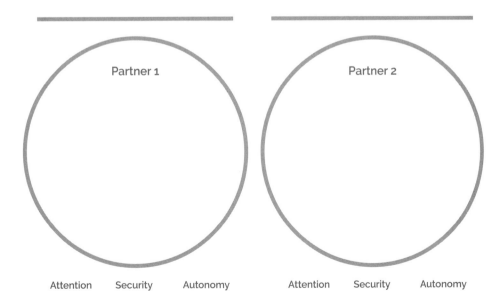

Questions

In what ways do you identify with the way your Enneagram triad processes information?

Partner 1:

Partner 2:

Are you and your partner in different triads? If so, identify some differences in how you each process information.

Partner 1:

Partner 2:

In a few sentences, write about a situation that you and your partner had a hard time seeing eye to eye on.

Partner 1:

Partner 2:

As you look back on that situation, what are some ways you were trying to protect and defend yourself through your triad?

Partner 1:

Partner 2:

With the new awareness you and your partner have regarding underlying issues of shame, anxiety, and anger, what are a few adjustments you would like to make in the way you communicate with one another?

Partner 1:

Partner 2:

Exploring the Stances

Brandon and Ella have been together for several years. The two of them grew up in very different environments. Brandon's parents were both present and engaged in his life. They ate dinner as a family and made it a priority to go to the children's sporting events and school activities. But Brandon's dad had strong opinions and desired for things to be done a certain way. The whole family understood these expectations and adapted to meet them. Because of this, Brandon was rarely asked to share his opinion, nor did he have space to explore new ways of doing things. Instead, he learned that in order to have a functional relationship, he needed to figure out what people expected and act accordingly. But what Brandon really wanted and still wants is to know that his voice matters and his feelings and ideas are worth exploring and being heard.

Ella, on the other hand, had parents who divorced when she was a toddler, and her mom worked full-time just trying to make ends meet. Ella had to help out around the house and do a lot of caretaking for herself and her younger sister. Her mother loved her and her sister fiercely, but she was not able to help with homework and rarely attended the girls' after-school activities because of her work schedule. Most days Ella came home to an empty house and had to find ways to entertain herself until her mom came home, and she loved having freedom. She liked making her own decisions, and she enjoyed helping her mom and sister. However, Ella also really wanted to know that she would be taken care of and that she was worth caring for.

As you can imagine, Brandon and Ella had very different expectations about what communication should look like within a romantic relationship. Ella loved hearing about Brandon's ideas and feelings, and Brandon was kind, compassionate, and understanding when Ella would talk about what she longed for in the future. But they didn't always respond to each other in a way that made sense. As time went on, they experienced frustration because of their differences. Ella expected Brandon to give her quick answers and be able to process his feelings on the spot. When he couldn't do that, it left her feeling anxious and burdensome. Brandon needed time to process what he was thinking and feeling so he could give Ella an honest answer. However, Ella's desire for an immediate response would overwhelm Brandon and cause him to retreat.

Once they began to unpack the Enneagram stances, Ella and Brandon found that they were each misunderstanding what the other person needed. Whenever Ella, a Seven, would naturally assert herself, Brandon, a Nine, would naturally withdraw. After learning about their differences, they were able to approach each other with compassion and understanding. They have since found a new rhythm of communication where they both feel safe, seen, and secure knowing they desire to hear and support one another in their life goals and decision-making.

· · · · · ·

As you can imagine, merging two people who have been raised in different environments can be not only challenging but at times downright exhausting. Each person has a different way of seeing the world, even if

Enneagram Stances

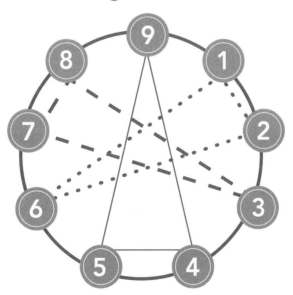

· · · ·
Compliant stance
Enneagram numbers 1, 2, and 6

───
Withdrawn stance
Enneagram numbers 4, 5, and 9

▬ ▬
Assertive stance
Enneagram numbers 3, 7, and 8

their beliefs, goals, and dreams are aligned. In fact, each Enneagram type has a specific stance that describes the way they interact with the world around them. Enneagram stances (also known as "Hornevian groups" or "social styles") are classified as assertive, compliant, or withdrawn.[8] Each Enneagram type's stance has been shaped by the encounters, conversations, and confrontations a person experienced during childhood. Stances reveal the "sense of self" that each Enneagram type unconsciously believes about themselves. When you become aware of your own perception of yourself, you will begin to unpack some of the deep-rooted tensions that exist within you. When you and your partner become aware of this information about each other, the conflicts within your relationship will come into focus.

Enneagram stances are directly connected to the way people thought they had to respond during childhood in order to get what they needed in a way that felt safe and effective. Understanding your and your partner's Enneagram stances will greatly impact the way you communicate with one another. Gaining knowledge and understanding about the different rhythms of response—immediate, delayed, or collective—will help the two of you communicate with fewer barriers and with deeper understanding, which will cause you both to be less defensive.

This type of awareness allows you to see your partner through eyes of compassion, care, and concern. You will not get as easily offended or frustrated, because you have a view into a deeper part of each other that helps you to grow in patience and self-control.

Let's take a closer look at the three Enneagram stances and how they impact the way you and your partner communicate.

Compliant Stance: Enneagram types One, Two, and Six believe at a subconscious level that it's their job to meet the demands and expectations of others. Individuals in the Compliant Stance look outside themselves to figure out who they should be and how they should act. Hoping to find stability and security, they move toward others. They ask questions, research, and explore their options. They also seek guidance and reassurance from people, organizations, and reputable sources in order to arrive at a decision they feel comfortable with. They form opinions and find security in the world around them by watching what others are doing and learning what is expected of them. They are more community-driven than people in the other stances.

Withdrawn Stance: Enneagram types Four, Five, and Nine believe at a subconscious level that they are not part of the group or that they don't fit in. People in the Withdrawn Stance gain their identity from moving away from others and retreating within themselves to process their experiences. They move away from others as a way to gain autonomy and allow themselves to reflect on what they really feel and think. They prefer to process their thoughts, opinions, and place in the world in the privacy of their own hearts and minds. Others can feel shut out because the person with a Withdrawn Stance needs to go inward to process. They can get lost in routines and numbing behaviors.

Assertive Stance: Enneagram types Three, Seven, and Eight believe at a subconscious level that everything meaningful that happens is in relation to them. Individuals in the Assertive Stance either move against or stand independently from others. At times they push against people to make their way in the world. This push is not necessarily intended to be aggressive; they just don't like it when things or people stand in the way of their goals. They are task-oriented, and they want to make an impact on the world. They are less aware of their impact on people around them and have a hard time connecting with their own feelings.

Here are some tips for using the stance information to enhance your relationship.

Compliant Stance

People in this stance need to know that they don't have to conform to other people's ideas to earn love and connection.

Encourage them to pursue their own dreams, reminding them of their worth through loving support.

Withdrawn Stance

People in this stance need to know that they don't have to retreat and withdraw for fear of being misunderstood or made to be quiet.

Encourage them to share their thoughts and ideas with you as you listen without trying to fix them.

Assertive Stance

People in this stance need to know that they don't have to demand
what they want because they are in a reciprocal relationship that
offers love, care, and nurture.

Encourage them to share their true feelings and thoughts without
condemning them or taking offense.

As you engage in the activity below, be mindful of the awareness you
have gained over the last several weeks. Learning about your Enneagram
stance has given you insight into how you take in information and process what you should do next in order to get what you want in life. This
information has the power to make you pause before you move forward
in certain situations.

Remember that just because you are in a particular stance doesn't mean
you have to be limited by that stance's coping strategies. Instead, you can
choose what is best for you moving forward because you now have the
knowledge of why you've been doing things this way all your life. This new
awareness also helps you relationally. Knowing and understanding the way
your partner processes information and deals with conflict allows you to
hold space for them in a new way. Instead of frustration and annoyance,
there can be understanding and communication.

Activity

In the image below, write your Enneagram stance on the line above your circle. Inside your circle, write down what you need as you process information according to your stance.

Examples:

"I need time to be able to figure out how I feel."

"I need my partner to look at me when I'm speaking."

"I need my partner to acknowledge the situation even if they can't agree with me."

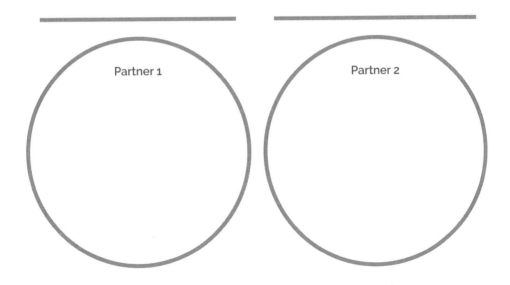

Questions

As you reflect on the information about your Enneagram stance, identify how that stance has caused you to respond to people, situations, and confrontation.

Partner 1:

Partner 2:

How would you describe the way you process information?

Partner 1:

Partner 2:

Write a few sentences about how you perceive your partner's stance. How does this information help you to understand and respect the way they process information?

Partner 1:

Partner 2:

Write three suggestions that will help you feel heard, seen, and understood.

Partner 1:

1. _____

2. _____

3. _____

Partner 2:

1. _____

2. _____

3. _____

WEEK 5

Overcoming Pitfalls

Signature Sins and Defense Mechanisms

> There is no greater agony than bearing an untold story inside of you.
>
> Maya Angelou

Conflict is inevitable, and so are pitfalls and misses within relationships. Life is full of ups and downs. Sometimes you'll feel like you're on top of the mountain and life is great. Other times you'll feel like you're in the valley and all will seem dim. The important thing is that you continue to communicate with your partner in all circumstances. Having open lines of communication and the freedom to approach each other about anything life throws your way will enable you both to feel safe and secure. This will build mutual trust and respect within your relationship where vulnerability feels safe. However, your defense mechanisms will tell you otherwise, and your signature sin will urge you to go after what you want without thinking about the effects of your decisions. That's why this week's content is so beneficial for you to know about each other.

As you continue to build upon the foundation being laid through awareness of the Enneagram system, you will find your eyes becoming open to your own patterns of behavior. As you each look at the *signature sin* for your

Enneagram number, you will see how that has distorted your thinking and caused you to chase what you believe will bring you satisfaction, comfort, and peace. As you and your partner explore your Enneagram number's *defense mechanism*, you will see the ways you have both tried to protect and defend yourselves throughout your life.

The thought patterns and behaviors you will explore this week stem from your core fear and your core desire. You have worked hard through the years to get your needs met, keep yourself safe, and receive love by using whatever means possible, even at your own expense and sometimes at the expense of your relationship.

Addressing Signature Sins

Bradley is a Four. He has always struggled with feeling like something within him is missing. He looks around at other people, and they just seem to have it easier than he does. He thinks to himself, "If I were a little more gifted, I would have gotten that promotion" or "If people didn't always misunderstand me, I wouldn't feel so insecure." Sometimes he even thinks, "If I were more driven, my wife, Angela, would have more respect for me." Bradley has become more aware of this thought pattern with the help of the Enneagram system. He has begun to understand how his insecurity is driven by his signature sin of envy. Bradley has to actively fight the lie that something within him is missing by using Scripture and prayer.

Gaining awareness of Bradley's signature sin has helped Angela better understand the struggle he faces. It also helps Angela to not take things personally. As an Eight, she's had to learn about her own signature sin, which is lust. As she has learned more about how this is displayed in her life, Angela has been able to better understand the tension points within their marriage. For an Eight, lust translates to intensity. Angela goes after what she desires with passion. She has a tendency to stir the pot and create chaos if she feels her environment is stale or boring. She has a lot of energy and at times will use it to get what she wants.

Over the years, whenever Bradley's insecurity encountered Angela's as-sertiveness, it caused fights that were hard to recover from. Through Enneagram awareness, they have both learned to not take things personally and to ask questions about what is really going on. They each have had to actively pursue the other and to speak to each other in loving, kind ways. They have learned what helps them to feel safe and secure in their relationship as well as what triggers their signature sins. Enneagram awareness has opened their eyes to what causes them to react and respond. They have become much more aware of their runaway emotions and what it is that they really need from each other. It has also helped them learn to communicate those needs in healthy and productive ways.

· · · · · · ·

Signature sins are best understood as a tendency to "miss the mark."[1] These nine sins or "passions" cause us to become trapped in unhealthy behavior patterns. The specific sin corresponding to your Enneagram number causes your thinking to become distorted. It misleads you into thinking you need more or you must hide parts of yourself, and it causes you to feel defeated and ultimately holds you back from achieving your true purpose. As you learn about your signature sin, you likely will have more understanding as to why you just can't seem to get things right sometimes. Exploring the pitfalls you typically find within your relationship will give you awareness and will position you to choose differently in the future. After all, walking through life oblivious to your weaknesses is like walking in the dark through a room full of obstacles. The great thing about Enneagram awareness is you no longer have to walk through life blind to your pitfalls and triggers. The Enneagram points out areas in your life where you are more susceptible and that lead to less-than-favorable situations.

Here is a list of the nine Enneagram types and their corresponding signature sin.

One = Anger

Ones believe anger is a wrong or bad emotion to express, so they typically try to hide it. They swallow anger as if it is a seed, and it tends to grow roots of bitterness and judgment. Anger can keep them from enjoying life and their many blessings because they are so focused on offenses.

Two = Pride

Twos pride themselves on not needing help and being the helper or savior to everyone. They are often unable to acknowledge their own pain and suffering. They tend to deny their own needs and focus on the needs of others. This keeps them from being vulnerable and transparent, which over time causes stress and tension within their relationships.

Three = Deceit

Threes often deceive themselves into thinking they are only as good as other people's opinions of them. This type of thinking causes them to chase after what will make them appear successful and give them a temporary high achieved through success. However, if they get caught up believing they are only what they do, they will neglect their relationships and lose out on a life filled with love and people.

Four = Envy

Fours feel as if something is fundamentally missing within them. They look at others and envy what they appear to have as far as skills and talents. In wishing they had the ability, talent, and skill of others, they often miss out on the many great gifts and talents they have within themselves.

Five = Greed

Fives store up for themselves the resources and knowledge they believe they will need for survival. They believe the world is a scary and unpredictable place, so it is best to never ask for help from others. They prefer to take care of their own needs and fear being depleted by others, so they withdraw and isolate, causing distance between themselves and others.

Six = Fear

Sixes often experience anxiety caused by fear because of the many unknowns in life. They are hypervigilant and apprehensive about the future. This causes them to miss out on what is happening in the present moment and not experience joy and peace.

Seven = Gluttony

Sevens are constantly in search of what will fill them up and satisfy them. They are like a bucket with holes in it—the more they fill it up, the more it runs out. They struggle to feel fully satisfied in life. Over time this constant chasing can lead to instability and loss.

Eight = Lust

Eights move toward intensity, passion, and control. They push everything in their lives to the extreme, hoping to feel fully alive and free. They assert themselves in an attempt to get what they want when they want it. Left unchecked, this type of behavior wears on relationships and friendships over time.

Nine = Sloth

Nines attempt to be unaffected by life. They are active yet disengaged from their activity. They desire to keep their environment harmonious, and they often do this by creating systems and rhythms that allow them to function on autopilot. Over time this behavior can cause distance and frustration within relationships.

Your signature sin is most likely not something you have been aware of. You might have realized you struggled with certain thought patterns or behaviors more than others but just chalked it up to "life is hard" or "this is just who I am." You might have repressed any acknowledgment of your passion because it makes you feel uncomfortable or ashamed or bad about yourself. Being blind to parts of yourself or keeping parts of yourself hidden means that there is most likely a difference between who you think you are (or who you would like to be seen as) and who you really are as you walk through life. However, when your signature sin remains hidden, it gains power and influence over your decisions, creating problems and greatly impacting your relationships.

Here are some warning signs for each Enneagram number that you are using your signature sin to get what you need and want. Check the boxes that you resonate with under your number and answer the questions that follow. Take your time with this section. Remember, you might not be conscious of this part of yourself, or it might be a part of yourself that you don't want to admit. Acknowledging your patterns allows for honesty, healing, and change.

Signs that your signature sin of ANGER is affecting your behavior as a One:

☐ You judge other people according to your standards.

☐ You say judgmental and sometimes rude comments about people who are different from you.

☐ You smile and act kind, yet internally you are really frustrated and mad.

☐ You are rigid and critical toward yourself.

Four questions to help you begin to uncover and discover how ANGER influences your decisions and creates problems that greatly impact your relationships:

1. In what ways does anger cause you to become triggered when fear arises in you?

2. What causes you to become angry and irritable?

3. Why do you tend to criticize yourself and others?

4. Are you able to clearly communicate your expectations to your partner?

Signs that your signature sin of PRIDE is affecting your behavior as a Two:

☐ You find yourself trying to please people at the expense of your own needs.

☐ You get angry and upset when you don't feel like you are wanted or valued.

☐ You feel guilty when you take time for yourself or treat yourself to something you have wanted.

☐ You remind others of all the things you have done for them so they understand the sacrifices you have made.

Four questions to help you begin to uncover and discover how PRIDE influences your decisions and creates problems that greatly impact your relationships:

1. What causes you to feel the need to go above and beyond for certain people?
2. What happens when you try to establish healthy boundaries?
3. Are you able to ask others for help without feeling guilt or shame?
4. What happens when you want to say no but don't feel like you can?

Signs that your signature sin of DECEIT is affecting your behavior as a Three:

☐ You want to quickly fix a situation, conversation, or person so you can move forward without dealing with feelings.

☐ When you have downtime, you feel anxious, nervous, and maybe even fearful that you will fall behind.

☐ You spend a lot of time cultivating an image that others will find attractive and engaging.

☐ You view every situation as a competition.

Four questions to help you begin to uncover and discover how DECEIT influences your decisions and creates problems that greatly impact your relationships:

1. What relationship issues are you having because you won't allow yourself to be open about your feelings?
2. How do you seek attention, and who do you seek it from?
3. What activities are you enjoying that have nothing to do with achievement or success?
4. What is behind your need to keep going even when you should slow down?

Signs that your signature sin of ENVY is affecting your behavior as a Four:

☐ You feel as though you are not as good as others or that others look down on you.

☐ You push people away to see if they will come back to you.

☐ You focus intently on the negative aspects of situations and give little attention to what is actually positive.

☐ You focus on being different, the black sheep of the family, or perhaps even outwardly rebellious as a form of self-protection rather than highlighting your positive traits.

Four questions to help you begin to uncover and discover how ENVY influences your decisions and creates problems that greatly impact your relationships:

1. What negative thoughts surface that often dictate how you feel about yourself?

2. How often do your emotions cause you to make up scenarios in your head about situations that may not be true?

3. What do you believe is missing inside you that causes you to not be able to engage in meaningful experiences or moments?

4. Do you suppress, overindulge, or ramp up your emotions as a way of dealing with difficult situations?

Signs that your signature sin of GREED is affecting your behavior as a Five:

☐ You feel that you don't need outside support, and because of that you tend to wall yourself off and try to live on as few resources as possible.

☐ You give little thought or attention to developing your own emotional well-being.

☐ You think that you don't have enough time or energy to give to anything or anyone else without depleting yourself.

☐ You feel detached from your emotions and seem to be watching your life from the sidelines.

Four questions to help you begin to uncover and discover how GREED influences your decisions and creates problems that greatly impact your relationships:

1. In what ways do you limit how much time you give to people or activities you feel are depleting you?
2. How do you detach from a situation because of the emotions it stirs in you?
3. In what ways do you try to control situations around you?
4. How do you react when people put expectations on you without speaking to you about them first?

Signs that your signature sin of FEAR is affecting your behavior as a Six:

☐ You believe you somehow deserve what is coming to you because of what you have or have not done.
☐ You are indecisive and unable to take action.
☐ You feel guilty and struggle with feelings of anxiety and fear.
☐ Your mind is overrun with catastrophic thinking.

Four questions to help you begin to uncover and discover how FEAR influences your decisions and creates problems that greatly impact your relationships:

1. How often do you find yourself scanning for danger or being hypervigilant?
2. How do you act out your fear through certain behaviors (e.g., irritability, aggression, being overly sensitive)?
3. How often do you blame others for situations and circumstances without looking at the role you may play in the story?
4. How have you witnessed yourself projecting your thoughts and feelings onto your partner?

Signs that your signature sin of GLUTTONY is affecting your behavior as a Seven:

☐ You constantly seek stimulation, adventure, and activity.

☐ You need to have options, so you have an exit strategy if situations become too difficult, intense, or boring.

☐ You feel the need to always be funny, happy-go-lucky, and outgoing so the environment is stimulating.

☐ You quickly move forward instead of processing a situation or circumstance that is heavy, hard, emotionally draining, or perhaps even devastating.

Four questions to help you begin to uncover and discover how GLUTTONY influences your decisions and creates problems that greatly impact your relationships:

1. In what ways do you seek pleasure as an avoidance of anything mundane, boring, or painful?

2. How do you react to people placing expectations or limitations on you?

3. Why do you focus on future activities and adventure rather than being present in the moment?

4. How do you respond when you find yourself in an uncomfortable situation?

Signs that your signature sin of LUST is affecting your behavior as an Eight:

☐ You believe your opinion is the right opinion without having all the data.

☐ You seek intensity by stirring up conflict to avoid feeling bored.

☐ You seek constant stimulation through fun and exciting experiences as a way to avoid feelings of emptiness, sadness, anxiety, or perhaps even confusion.

☐ You struggle with impulsivity and indulging yourself to avoid difficult situations or feelings.

Four questions to help you begin to uncover and discover how LUST influences your decisions and creates problems that greatly impact your relationships:

1. Why do you tend to deny your internal and external limitations?
2. Why do you think you focus on acting from power and strength?
3. What causes you to want to move into action instead of slowing down and processing the situation?
4. Why do you think you avoid relying on others or allowing yourself to be vulnerable?

Signs that your signature sin of SLOTH is affecting your behavior as a Nine:

☐ You become passive-aggressive.

☐ You find yourself procrastinating.

☐ You become irritable and stubborn.

☐ You know you need to find a job, change jobs, or get out of a relationship, yet you don't take any action toward change.

Four questions to help you begin to uncover and discover how SLOTH influences your decisions and creates problems that greatly impact your relationships:

1. How often do you forget about yourself and go along with what others want to do?
2. What types of conversations, relationships, and situations cause you to withdraw from people?
3. How often do you find yourself stuck, sitting still, or procrastinating when it pertains to your own needs, wants, and desires?
4. How difficult is it for you to make small decisions about what you want?

Slowing down and allowing yourself to sit and process the above information will help you to uncover and discover when and how your signature sin calls to you. Your signature sin has a way of luring you into thinking and acting in ways that do not serve you well. It desires to draw you by trying to give you what will make you feel good in the moment but often leaves you with regret and frustration.

Activity

In this activity, write the signature sin for your Enneagram type on the line above your circle. Inside your circle, write down the ways you can identify how you have used your sin. Choose a different color pen and write a sentence that describes how you will put boundaries around your signature sin and make an effort to choose differently. (Example: "As a Seven, when I feel the need to fill myself up by overspending, I will instead ask myself what it is I really need.")

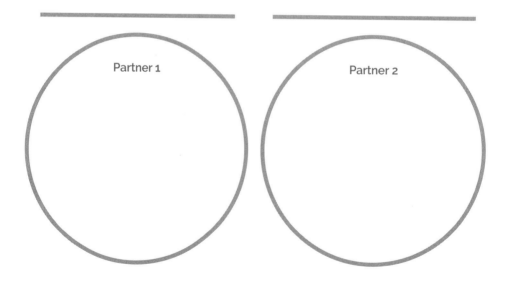

Partner 1   Partner 2

Questions

How does your signature sin express itself in your life?

Partner 1:

Partner 2:

What effects has your signature sin had on your relationships in the past?

Partner 1:

Partner 2:

How has your signature sin shown up in your attempts to meet your needs throughout your life?

Partner 1:

Partner 2:

Recognizing Defense Mechanisms

Anthony and Aliyah have been married for several years. They met in high school and have been side by side ever since. They both have extremely stressful jobs and have been trying to have a baby for the past two years. Anthony, an Eight, often feels overwhelmed by the demands of his job and the expectations at home. He finds that he tends to deny his role in the fighting that unfolds. He puts a lot of the blame on Aliyah, feeling like she just doesn't understand the weight that he is carrying. At times he gets loud and aggressive, slamming doors and cabinets, but underneath these feelings, he is really afraid that Aliyah is just disappointed because he works long hours and can't seem to give her what she so badly wants—a baby.

Aliyah, a Four, is often overwhelmed by her emotions and tends to feel alone in her longing to become a mom. She is a nurse and spends her days caring for others. When she gets home, she wants to be met by a husband who sees the beauty in her and desires to spend time with her. However, she often comes home to an empty house and eats dinner alone in front of the television. She wishes so badly that Anthony would see her pain and her desire for him to be her partner in life and love. When she expresses her desire for Anthony to be more attentive and present, he spins it back on her, blaming her for being too needy and demanding. This, in turn, causes her to shrink back and share less. She immediately takes his comments into herself and begins to believe her needs are just too great and she is being unrealistic.

This cycle of fighting was the catalyst that pushed Anthony and Aliyah to begin exploring their Enneagram numbers. They wanted to try to understand what was really happening below the surface of their reactions. As they unpacked their defense mechanisms, they began to realize why they were missing each other so often. They both loved each other and wanted the very same thing—a baby. They just had a hard time getting on the same page. They were like trains going in the same direction but on different tracks.

As they began to understand their own defense mechanisms, they could better resist the urge to respond the way they always had. They began to move toward each other in their stress, hurt, and longing. They realized they both wanted the same thing, and to get on the same train they had to communicate without allowing their defense mechanisms to get the best of them. They now start hard conversations with this phrase: "The story I am telling myself about this situation is . . ."

They learned to listen in order to hear one another instead of listening to respond. They began to understand the importance of each other's heart longing messages. This allowed them to be more empathetic and compassionate toward each other. The knowledge they have gained from Enneagram awareness has taught them how to live life on the same train, going in the same direction, pursuing the same goals and desires for their family. It has been life-changing and has brought them together in a more loving and supportive way.

· · · · · ·

Defense mechanisms are unconscious coping strategies we use to help deal with uncomfortable and difficult situations. These strategies operate at an unconscious level and help us deal with sadness, anxiety, anger, shame, and other emotions. Defense mechanisms are natural and normal and are used to help us maintain our self-image and personal boundaries.

Defense Mechanisms

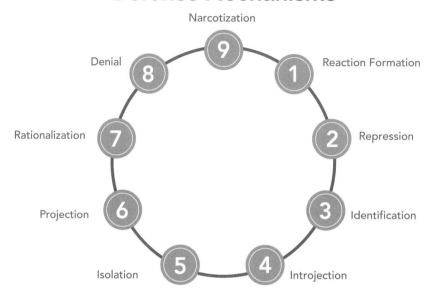

However, when they become overused, our defense mechanisms can cause such things as phobias, obsessions, and severe anxiety.

Marriage brings out the best and the worst in us. In marriage, we come face-to-face with parts of ourselves that we have been able to keep hidden from most people. Defense mechanisms are one way we keep our more vulnerable side from getting hurt, rejected, or betrayed. In a healthy and stable committed relationship, we use our defense mechanisms to cope throughout life, giving valuable insight into our behavior patterns. We don't just do things because that is who we are. We do things because that is how we learned to protect ourselves from a very young age.

Here's one example of what this looks like. A person who is a Seven avoids difficult situations and feelings of sadness, fear, anxiety, and loneliness by reframing them from a more positive perspective. In their mind, they believe that people like to be around happy, upbeat people, so the safest way to protect themselves is to avoid their lower emotions. Over time, however, avoiding difficult feelings causes the Seven to hide parts of themselves, and living in the reality of their own life can seem impossible. This is where the Seven's signature sin of gluttony comes in and whispers lies that they just need more of whatever brings relief or temporary happiness. At the end of the day, the only way to truly find relief and happiness is to face reality, allow the emotions to surface, and feel the feelings.

When we are in a safe and secure relationship, our partner can become a great support as we face parts of ourselves that have been our method of coping. We may think our defense mechanisms are helping us, but in reality they keep us from the freedom we seek to be loved, valued, cared for, and connected to our partner through vulnerability and trust.

Below are descriptions of the defense mechanism for each Enneagram type and an example of how each could play out in marriage.

One = Reaction Formation

To try reducing or eliminating anxiety caused by their own thoughts, feelings, or behaviors that they consider unacceptable, Ones respond in the exact opposite way from their real feelings. Their inner critic dictates what is acceptable based on social norms, their environment, and moral principles. In extreme cases, Ones may voice disapproval of a person or situation and then later be caught acting in the same way or participating in something corrupt.

Chad is a One. He is very particular in the way he likes the garage organized and kept. Shannon, his wife, is a Nine, and she tries to help keep things orderly and peaceful. At times she takes the initiative and moves things around in the garage, trying to help keep things clean and tidy. This drives Chad crazy, yet he often thanks Shannon for helping him and then heads to the garage and moves things back to the way he had them. He feels like it's not okay to express his frustration and anger about Shannon's help because that would make him look like an unappreciative jerk. However, as Chad learned to explain his thought processes and expectations to Shannon, it helped them with communication and connection.

Two = Repression

Twos try to hide from themselves by focusing on others' needs instead of acknowledging their own. They may suppress feelings, desires, wishes, fears, and needs that are too difficult or perhaps seem too overwhelming to consciously admit. But try as they might to repress them, feelings don't just disappear. Instead, Twos express them through passive-aggressive or aggressive behavior, nitpicking, clinginess, and manipulation. They often try to reassure others who are dealing with the same issues they have dealt with or are still dealing with to unconsciously heal themselves.

Jessica is a Two. She is a loving, caring, nurturing woman who tries to meet the needs of those she loves by anticipating what is about to happen and making sure everyone has what they need. She does this from a place of love; however, she has a hard time recognizing her own needs and wants. Jessica will rarely speak about her needs for fear of being seen as needy. She expects her loved ones—particularly her husband, Scott, and her close friends—to automatically know what she needs because, after all, she does that for all of them.

Scott, a Five, finds himself overwhelmed by Jessica's constant awareness of needs and her seeming disappointment in his inability to truly see her and what she desires. Scott often retreats into his own space because he has a hard time figuring out how to emotionally support Jessica. This causes Jessica to internalize thoughts like "After everything I do for you, you still can't seem to show up for me" or "If you really loved me, you would know what I need right now." These thoughts often create a wedge between her and Scott, and they find themselves living in silent distance from one another. However, as Jessica began to recognize when she was suppressing her feelings and thoughts, she was able to share what she needed in a way that was clear for Scott to receive. This has allowed her expectations to be met, and movement toward each other has brought connection and fulfillment.

Three = Identification

Threes unconsciously incorporate attributes and characteristics of another person into their own personality and sense of self. They usually are not even aware that they have created a false persona, and it can be hard for them to untangle from this pattern. Threes tend to build their self-esteem by forming a real or imaginary alliance with someone they admire, to the extent that they take on that person's characteristics and desire to be just like them.

Matthew is a Three. He is incredibly driven and constantly looks for ways to improve himself so he can continue to move up in his company. When he started playing golf with a few of the executives from his office, Matthew's wife, Heidi, noticed his language and clothing style began to change. She witnessed Matthew speaking down to a waitress at the restaurant and his sudden desire to have a particular brand of golf clubs. When Heidi brought this up to Matthew, he was defensive and dismissive. He did not think she was right, and he felt like she was trying to control him. Heidi is a Six, and she was simply observing that the changes her husband was displaying were concerning to her. She didn't want to lose the fun, adventurous, generous, kind man she married. However, as Matthew began to learn about his Enneagram defense mechanism and the reasons why he adapted and enmeshed, he could see what Heidi was talking about. He has since made it a point to pay attention to how he is acting and responding to the people and situations around him. He also asks Heidi to tell him if she sees him adapting and enmeshing and losing himself.

Four = Introjection

Fours fully absorb critical information and negative experiences instead of expelling them. They internalize and incorporate negative perceptions while repelling any positive feedback they have been given. In that way, they prefer to deal with self-inflicted damage rather than respond to criticism or rejection from others.

Micah is a Four. He often feels overwhelmed and irritated by what he perceives as other people's lack of emotional intelligence. He can't tolerate people who don't attempt to understand how their words will impact others. He has been on the receiving end of comments and compliments that he does not feel he can fully trust. His wife, Stephanie, is a One. She often tells Micah she is proud of him but then follows that up with ways he can improve. He can't help but immediately dismiss her compliments because all he hears is what he doesn't do right or well. However, as Micah has felt safe enough to share with Stephanie that he has a hard time receiving compliments when they are sandwiched between correction or suggested improvements, she has been able to better understand why her words of encouragement always seemed to cause a fight.

Five = Isolation

Fives isolate themselves as a way to avoid becoming overwhelmed or depleted. They go into their minds and cut themselves off from their feelings. They compartmentalize each part of themselves from their whole self as a way of coping with overwhelming feelings and expectations.

Sam is a Five. He is very structured and dislikes when his time is interrupted or his space is invaded. He has a hard time openly showing his emotions and often retreats into his man cave to avoid having any expectations put on him. He withdraws because he doesn't feel like he can meet his wife's expectations and hates to see the look on her face when he fails. His wife, Megan, is an Eight and tends to tell Sam what he needs to do and what she needs from him in a matter-of-fact way. Sam loves that Megan is strong and assertive, but sometimes it can feel overwhelming when she invades his space or makes plans and springs them on him. However, as Sam has worked on better communication through Enneagram awareness, he has been able to share with Megan what he needs as far as space, timeline, and expectations. This has caused a closeness within their relationship that they didn't know was possible.

Six = Projection

Sixes unconsciously attribute their own unacceptable, unwanted, or disowned thoughts, emotions, feelings, motivations, characteristics, and behaviors onto others. They do this because they find these things difficult to acknowledge or threatening to believe about themselves. They think they are creating safety and security using this defense mechanism; however, it often leads to heightened anxiety. Sixes tend to create a false reality by believing the stories they invent in their minds.

Sarah is a Six. She is family-oriented, funny, and full of energy. She loves to plan gatherings and have all her people together. At times she gets frustrated by other people's opinions and suggestions, and she will often project those frustrations onto her husband, Will, who is a Three. Sarah tends to spin her frustration and feelings as if they are Will's, and he is left feeling defeated and doesn't know how to respond. So Will becomes quiet and withdrawn, which then leads Sarah to feel more frustration and irritation. Harmful words are spoken, and repairing the relationship takes longer and longer each time it happens. However, as Sarah has learned Enneagram awareness, she now starts a conversation with Will by saying, "The story I am telling myself is . . ." or "Even though I feel this way about the situation, how are you feeling?" This allows Sarah and Will to speak their personal truth and own their individual stories.

Seven = Rationalization

Sevens explain their unacceptable thoughts, feelings, and behaviors in a way that obscures or altogether avoids their true motivations and intentions and any consequences. They do this by positive reframing of situations and emotions to avoid pain, discomfort, sadness, guilt, and anxiety. They also do this to justify their selfish behaviors and avoid taking personal responsibility for their negative actions.

Hannah is a Seven. She has a positive, upbeat demeanor and doesn't let things bother her. She sometimes overbooks herself and loses track of her personal responsibilities, and things at home don't get done, like paying the bills on time. This drives her husband, Brad, crazy. Brad is a Three, and he tries to tell Hannah to schedule the payments or put a reminder on her phone, but she just shrugs and dismisses his ideas. Hannah's positive reframing allows her to not take full responsibility for her actions, and this is causing major tension within their marriage. However, as Hannah has begun to use her Enneagram awareness and allowed herself to recognize when she is reframing, she has begun to take responsibility for her actions and set some order and predictability in her life.

Eight = Denial

Eights unconsciously negate anything that makes them feel anxious by simply acting like it never existed. This can come in many forms, such as dismissing thoughts, feelings, wishes, sensations, and even their own needs. They may deny the reality of the unpleasant information altogether. They may acknowledge the information but deny the severity of it. Or they may even acknowledge the information and its severity but deny their involvement in it.

Chris, an Eight, is strong, competent, and driven. He moves at a fast pace and tends to step into situations before they have been fully vetted. He often blames others for what goes wrong and doesn't see the part he has played in the problem. His wife, Becky, who is a Nine, has learned to navigate this by avoiding conversations that would bring up the issue of fault, but this has caused a lot of distance and silence in their marriage. Becky doesn't like to be on the receiving end of Chris's frustration, and Chris doesn't like to be on the receiving end of Becky's correction, so silence has become the norm within their relationship. However, through Enneagram awareness, Chris has begun to recognize his pattern of pushing blame away from himself and has begun to ask questions like "What part do I need to own in this story?" and "What is true about the story I am telling myself?" This new pattern has changed his relationship with Becky, allowing for conversation and emotional connection.

Nine = Narcotization

Nines try to numb themselves to avoid anything that feels too large, complex, difficult, or uncomfortable to handle. They do this by engaging in long, rhythmic activities that are familiar, require very little attention, and provide comfort, such as watching television, taking long naps, doing yard work, reading a book, going for a walk, or engaging in extended casual conversation. They also like to have a daily routine, such as a morning and night ritual that allows them to go through the motions and not be fully present.

Alexa is a Nine. She is easygoing, kindhearted, and gentle. She doesn't like chaos, loud noises, or unpredictable outcomes. She has a way of doing things that enables her to stay calm, cool, and collected at all times. Her husband, Mark, is a Seven. He has a way of stirring energy and livening up the environment by simply being himself, which at times causes Alexa to retreat into her own headspace and get lost in chores or a book. Early on, Mark's loud and extroverted spirit drew Alexa to him, and she felt intoxicated by his energy and excitement. But after a few years of marriage, the novelty of it has worn off. She now finds herself annoyed by his big personality and his desire to go, go, go. However, through Enneagram awareness, Alexa has begun expressing her need for peace and order by sharing with Mark how overwhelmed she sometimes feels by his sudden plans and abrupt changes. She also works on laying out what it looks like for her to be able to be more spontaneous so she can enjoy her husband and the fun he brings to her life.

. . . . . .

As you seek greater Enneagram awareness, here are four steps to help you recognize what you need to overcome the childhood patterns of behavior that trigger your defense mechanisms and coping strategies.

First, allow yourself to look back at your childhood and recognize what you needed to feel connected, loved, and supported. Share your findings with your partner and talk about the ways they can give you connection, love, and support within your relationship.

Second, think about the disciplines you need to establish in your life that can help you let your guard down and feel safe and secure with your partner. Share your thoughts with your partner and come up with a plan that supports the new disciplines you'd like to establish.

Third, make a list of activities that evoke feelings of joy and happiness inside of you. Share your list with your partner and make plans to participate in life-giving experiences together.

Fourth, be honest with yourself about what you need to feel renewed and rested. Share with your partner what you believe helps you to live your life filled up and at ease—for example, exercising or time alone. Then talk about how they can support you in these activities.

As you and your partner allow yourselves to be more vulnerable and open with each other, remember that we can give others only what we have practiced giving ourselves. The work you are doing is both independent and collaborative. When you both actively show up for yourselves and participate in the work of awareness, you will be better able to hold space for each other as you establish new rhythms and patterns of behavior.

========= *Activity* =========

Take some time and review the defense mechanism for your Enneagram number. Ask yourself the following questions:

"What causes me to feel I must protect myself?"

"How do I react when I feel I must protect myself?"

"How have I learned to cope according to my Enneagram defense mechanism?"

In the image below, the stick figure represents you and the circle represents all the things that cause your defense mechanism to be activated. Fill in your circle with words or phrases that trigger your defense mechanism. These could include:

A person	An item	A smell	A look
A place	A sound	A phrase	

Partner 1

Partner 2

Questions

In what ways have you witnessed your defense mechanism being used as a coping strategy in your life?

Partner 1:

Partner 2:

In what ways has your defense mechanism caused you to guard yourself or disconnect in your relationship?

Partner 1:

Partner 2:

Now that you and your partner have awareness of each other's defense mechanism and coping strategy, what new patterns of behavior need to be developed to help you support one another and move toward each other for connection?

Partner 1:

Partner 2:

List two ways your partner can show you that they can be trusted enough to let your guard down and share your vulnerabilities.

Partner 1:

Partner 2:

WEEK 6

Building a Solid Connection through Security and Love

Stress and Growth Patterns

Nothing can bring a real sense of security into the home except true love.

Billy Graham

Love is a word that carries a lot of weight. To love someone means you feel profoundly tender toward them. It also means you have a passionate affection for them, which causes you to have feelings of warm personal attachment and deep connection. Love also drives you toward a sexual passion or desire for your partner, which brings you together in an intimate way that is exclusive to just the two of you. Security within a relationship means that you feel safe with your partner. You're able to trust them, and this allows you to let your guard down and release feelings of anxiety, worry, and fear. A healthy relationship requires both partners to extend love, security, and trust to one another so they can build a solid connection on a firm foundation.

Stress is inevitable, but when you have a relationship that permits open communication and acceptance, you will find you can overcome so much in life because you feel safe, seen, loved, and secure. For each Enneagram number, there is a *stress point* the person moves toward when they are anxious, exhausted, frustrated, stressed, burdened, or overwhelmed. When you and your partner attempt to reestablish boundaries and order, or when you attempt to gain control over your feelings, emotions, and thoughts, you will often act out the unhealthy traits of your stress point number. Your stress point characteristics tend to be the opposite characteristics of your true Enneagram number.

But each Enneagram number also has a *growth point* that a person moves toward as they uncover and discover healthy patterns of behavior. As an individual develops good mental, emotional, and relational habits, they begin to adjust their patterns of behavior and apply healthy coping strategies that give them long-term positive benefits. Even though your main Enneagram number never changes because your core motivations are always attached to your unconscious childhood messages and heart longing messages, you will learn to incorporate the healthy characteristics of your growth number into your main number and become a more well-rounded and high-functioning human being.

Understanding Stress Patterns

Max, a Seven, is full of vision and passion. He has lots of ideas and the energy to make them happen. He often fills his calendar with social gatherings and fun outings. He likes to be on the go, but his business tends to cause him to overcommit and underdeliver. When Max becomes stressed, he starts to display some of the average and unhealthy behaviors of a One. (For more detailed descriptions of healthy, average, and unhealthy behaviors for each Enneagram type, see appendix B.) He becomes rigid and restrictive with himself and tries to control the people and situations that directly affect him. He loses his fun-loving side and becomes serious and structured.

Max is married to Lilly, who is a One. Lilly has repeatedly told Max that she feels overlooked and unimportant to him because he is always going out with his friends or planning couples dinners. Lilly just really wants Max's attention, but he feels smothered and controlled by her needs. Lilly, who is usually levelheaded and orderly, finds herself gravitating toward the average to unhealthy side of a Four. As she becomes more stressed and exhausted, she becomes moody and withdrawn. She fantasizes about how the relationship could be and the love and longing she wishes Max had for her. If she and Max ignore each other's bids for connection, Max will put up a wall to protect himself from rejection. That will continue to keep Lilly at arm's length, which has the potential to spiral her into depression.

As Max becomes more aware of his strengths and weaknesses and his heart longing message, he can recognize his unhealthy patterns and ask himself why he is acting this way and what he is gaining from this behavior. He has the opportunity to recognize how his actions suggest that others are more important than Lilly and to make sure that he gives her priority in his life. Showing her how much she means to him and why he chose her to be his wife will help him to make choices that put her and their relationship first.

As Lilly becomes more aware of her strengths and weaknesses and her heart longing message, she has the ability to recognize her unhealthy patterns and to think about how she can show up for herself and speak the truth. She is able to communicate her needs and desires without the fear of looking bad or needy, and she knows that Max sees her and loves her.

Lilly and Max are learning to make and accept bids of connection from each other. They are learning about the importance of a healthy rhythm within their home and social schedule, and of balancing time together and time with friends and loved ones. Each day is a new day to choose healthy communication and love toward each other.

· · · · · ·

Let's take a closer look at stress. Stress is a state of mental tension and worry caused by problems in your life, work, and relationships. Everyone experiences stress and stressors on a daily basis. The things that cause you stress may not be the same things that cause your spouse stress, and vice versa. Stress is an indicator that something is off in your life, such as a lack of boundaries or a violation of boundaries. Stress is also triggered when you have little to no margin in your life. Margin is essential for your health and well-being.

Establishing healthy boundaries and a healthy rhythm in your life allows you to cut down on stress and function from a place of awareness and margin. You no longer allow life to just happen to you; instead, you take an active role in how your life unfolds. You begin to realize that for everything you say yes to, you are saying no to something else. When you are stressed out, have little margin, or don't have healthy boundaries in place, it's easy to miss bids of connection, which are ways your partner tries to connect with you. A bid for connection might sound like, "Larry, did you see the movie trailer with our favorite actor in it?" Larry then has an opportunity to turn toward his partner and say something like, "Yes, babe, I did. Do you want to go see the movie this weekend?" This is a healthy and positive response to a bid for connection. If Larry chose not to respond or simply said no, he would have missed a bid for connection his partner was trying to have with him. A bid for connection can also be nonverbal and might look like your partner gently placing their hand on your lower back or perhaps even giving a little love tap on your bottom as they walk by.

Your ability to lean into a bid your partner is extending will help you grow closer together. If you don't have margin and you're overly stressed, there's a good chance you will miss the bids for connection that your partner is extending toward you. A lack of margin and clear boundaries will drive your stress level up, leaving you bogged down by the weight of work, other people's expectations, and decreased time and energy. Margin and boundaries are the building blocks for a healthy life and an emotionally connected couple who respond to each other's bids for connection.

Enneagram Numbers under Stress

1 goes to 4 in stress	4 goes to 2 in stress	7 goes to 1 in stress
2 goes to 8 in stress	5 goes to 7 in stress	8 goes to 5 in stress
3 goes to 9 in stress	6 goes to 3 in stress	9 goes to 6 in stress

Stress Points

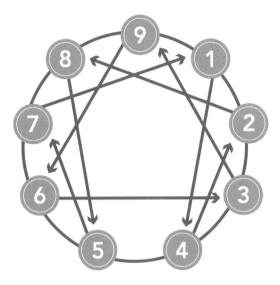

An average to unhealthy **One** under stress will act out the average to unhealthy traits of a **Four**. They become moody, sensing others do not take them or their values seriously. They tend to become resentful of others and may even feel misunderstood, so they withdraw to sort out their feelings alone. If the One stays in a stressful state for a prolonged amount of time, they may become isolated, which can lead to depression. In trying to make themselves feel better, they may become self-indulgent, which will only perpetuate the cycle of stress in their life.

An average to unhealthy **Two** under stress will act out the average to unhealthy traits of an **Eight**. They become resentful if they feel rejected or overlooked by others. They tend to become controlling and dominating, often telling people what to do and how to do it. They can have outbursts, be confrontational, or even threaten to withdraw support from others when they are feeling stressed or threatened. To get attention, they may also position themselves to be at the center of situations.

An average to unhealthy **Three** under stress will act out the average to unhealthy traits of a **Nine**. They turn on autopilot, hoping to get through situations without being affected by them. They tend to lose their focus and drive, and if the stress is prolonged, they may become listless and completely shut down. They may struggle with depression and begin to withdraw from people and projects. They may get to a place where they no longer have the energy or enthusiasm to keep up the appearance of happiness, hoping others will leave them alone and give them space.

An average to unhealthy **Four** under stress will act out the average to unhealthy traits of a **Two**. They defend their hurt feelings by withdrawing from people or withholding affection and attention. They become clingy when they feel they are losing connection and may overcompensate by creating dependencies or even using manipulation to try and win others over. They tend to remind others of how much they are needed and how much support they have given to them. They become more possessive of loved ones, not wanting to let them out of their sight.

An average to unhealthy **Five** under stress will act out the average to unhealthy traits of a **Seven**. They become nervous and high-strung. Their minds begin to jump from one thing to another, causing them to feel scattered, distracted, and out of control. They can become restless and hyperactive, suddenly taking on projects and overcommitting themselves. They may also become very talkative, impulsive, and flighty.

An average to unhealthy **Six** under stress will act out the average to unhealthy traits of a **Three**. They jump into action and put on a persona to deal with their anxieties. They tend to act as if everything is okay, even when they feel overwhelmed. They become task-oriented and highly efficient, trying to create order to calm their anxieties. They may shut down their feelings so they are able to be more productive, or they may become emotionally unstable and unable to complete tasks.

An average to unhealthy **Seven** under stress will act out the average to unhealthy traits of a **One**. They become hypercritical of themselves and others. They try to rein themselves in and become more disciplined. They tend to become easily frustrated, impatient, and irritable with themselves and others. They may feel trapped and restricted as they attempt to establish order in their life. They may become harsh and perfectionistic toward themselves and others when they are under a time crunch or feel they can't meet expectations.

An average to unhealthy **Eight** under stress will act out the average to unhealthy traits of a **Five**. They retreat from others and seek isolation as a way to process their thoughts and feelings. They pull back from situations to assess how they can regain control. They may become unusually quiet, secretive, and isolated while they process how to deal with difficult thoughts, feelings, emotions, and situations. If they are under prolonged periods of stress, they may become cynical toward themselves, others, and life in general.

An average to unhealthy **Nine** under stress will act out the average to unhealthy traits of a **Six**. They tend to become worried, testy, defensive, and paranoid. They begin to see people as their source of frustration. They may complain to anyone who will listen, and they will blame everyone else for their own distress. They may have outbursts of frustration with people whom they feel are trying to control or manipulate them.

Activity

Think back to the last time you felt stressed and can recognize your Enneagram number moving toward your stress number based on behaviors. In the list below, circle the emotions that surfaced when you felt stressed.

Abandoned	Anxious	Confused
Accused	Ashamed	Criticized
Alienated	Attacked	Demeaned
Alone	Belittled	Despair
Angry	Betrayed	Disappointed

Dumb	Hurt	Powerless
Embarrassed	Inadequate	Rejected
Empty	Insignificant	Small
Failure	Invisible	Terrified
Foolish	Irritable	Timid
Frustrated	Lonely	Unacceptable
Guilty	Lost	Unloved
Helpless	Misunderstood	Unwanted
Hopeless	Numb	Vulnerable
Humiliated	Panicky	Worthless

Write a sentence explaining how you felt for the three most accurate words that you circled. Example: "I felt alone when my stress level escalated, causing me to react to everyone as if they were the problem."

Review the sentences you have written, and for each one ask yourself, "Is this true?" Are the thoughts that surface about the people and the situation true, or is the stress activating your fears and causing you to become defensive and self-protective?

· · · · · ·

Here are the warning signs for each Enneagram type when a person is moving toward their stress number:

One: When I am stressed, I become irritable and frustrated.

Two: When I am stressed, I become pushy and demanding.

Three: When I am stressed, I become disconnected and aloof.

Four: When I am stressed, I become clingy and excessively needy.

Five: When I am stressed, I become scattered and look for ways to escape.

Six: When I am stressed, I become driven and task-oriented.

Seven: When I am stressed, I become hypercritical.

Eight: When I am stressed, I become withdrawn and secretive.

Nine: When I am stressed, I become worried and passive-aggressive.

Taking your time and participating in the next activity will help you put words to your feelings and behaviors. Once you recognize your patterns, you have the power to change them. You have to allow yourself to feel what it is you're feeling in order to heal and move forward. When you attempt to push through your emotions, they don't just disappear. Instead, they get pushed down inside of you and then bubble up as anxiety, frustration, irritability, and even rage. It's worth your time to investigate what causes you stress so you can learn from it and grow.

Activity

On the line above your circle, write down which Enneagram number you move toward when you are stressed.

Inside your circle, write down words that describe the ways you behave under stress (e.g., nitpicky, aggressive, withdrawn).

Under your circle write down the ways your partner can support you when you are under stress. (Examples: "Sit with me." "Hold my hand." "Listen to me without trying to fix me.")

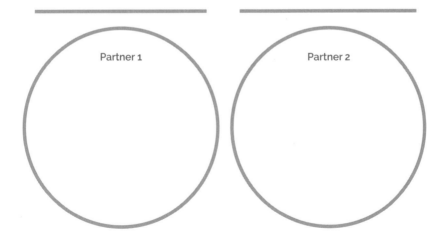

151

Questions

What are a few things you have learned about the stress point for your Enneagram type and the effects it has on you?

Partner 1:

Partner 2:

How has gaining awareness about your stress point helped you to better understand your behaviors?

Partner 1:

Partner 2:

What are a few things your partner can do to help you when they notice you are acting from your stress point?

Partner 1:

Partner 2:

Write down a way you plan on supporting your partner now that you have a better understanding of their stress point behavior.

Partner 1:

Partner 2:

——————————— **Embracing Growth Points** ———————————

Eric, an Enneagram Six, has been working hard to recognize his patterns of behavior. He really desires to move toward his growth number, which is a Nine. He wants to worry less and enjoy his new married life with his wife, Amanda. Amanda is a Two, and she often feels nervous to share her true feelings and needs with Eric. She doesn't want to overwhelm or burden him with her fears and desires. However, she has been doing her own work around Enneagram awareness, and she knows that the best way for them to build a solid foundation in their marriage is with honesty and transparency. She is actively working on moving toward a Four, which is where she moves to in health and growth. She is understanding the importance of honest communication and voicing expectations. Eric and Amanda are both becoming aware of their stress triggers, as well as what moves them toward health and growth. They have found that consistency and rhythm, as well as margin and healthy boundaries, allow them to feel loved and secure within their relationship.

As you become more aware of your own patterns of behavior, you will embark on a new chapter of your life. You will begin exploring what you want for your life from a healthy, self-aware state. The road to health and growth is not about your old patterns of behavior; instead, it is about choosing a path that you desire and establishing healthy behavior patterns and rhythms to support these changes. When you begin to feel the desire to show up for yourself in a real and authentic way and start seeking different ways of doing things, you are on your way to growth. The key is to stop believing "this is just who I am" and instead start asking, "Will this get me where I want to go so I'm the healthiest version of myself?" As you learn to become more present and aware of what you are thinking, feeling, and sensing, you will find growth to be a natural choice. And when you pair this with a healthy relationship, trust, love, and support are inevitable.

Three Facets of Health

Health is defined as "a state of complete physical, mental, and social well-being and not merely the absence of disease or infirmity."[1] In order to move toward health and growth in your own personal life, you must look at the three components of growth: physical, mental, and social. Each person is responsible for their own physical, mental, and social well-being, but people often feel the need to take on responsibility for their partner's happiness. It is not your job to make your partner happy and satisfied in life. It is each person's own responsibility to discover what makes them feel fulfilled, at peace, confident, and satisfied in life.

Physical health is one important aspect of finding satisfaction and fulfillment in life. This is because physical exercise releases the neurotransmitters dopamine and serotonin, which help relieve stress and anxiety and improve mood and sleep patterns. If you're a person who enjoys physical activity and has a good routine, I encourage you to continue in that. If you're a person who dreads physical activity or perhaps hasn't given it much thought, I encourage you to find something you enjoy and start making it a priority in your life. Consistency is key. You don't have to hit the gym five days a week; instead, try doing something three days a week that elevates your heart rate and causes you to sweat a little. The focus of physical activity for mental health is not to be skinnier, prettier, or physically fit. It is about releasing stress and taking a little time to value yourself and honor your body.

Mental health is so important yet often not clearly understood. In the same way that your physical body needs both work and rest, your mind and soul need to have both challenge and rest. Balancing your mental health requires self-care. Self-care is simply allowing yourself the time to address what your body and mind need in a way that centers on peace and restoration. Moving toward growth means you begin to understand that stress is often unavoidable and that it's important for you to engage in activities that help reduce stress, such as physical movement, meditation, a warm bath, or even a massage.

Allowing yourself to focus on self-care will help you be more in tune to the relational needs within your marriage. You will be more likely to engage in your relationship from a place of wholeness because you have intentionally done your own work. You will no longer expect your partner to fulfill or complete you, because you will understand that it's impossible for another human being to do that. You will recognize that you have a choice about how you react to the stress of this world. By actively learning what your body and mind need, such as spiritual disciplines, prayer, adequate rest, exercise, and healthy food choices, you will be more prepared to care for your partner and to work on cultivating a relationship that is full of possibilities and love.

Social well-being is tied to meaningful social relationships and connections. As you move toward your growth number, you will begin to open yourself more to healthy relationships and communication. You and your partner will learn words, gestures, and phrases that bring comfort and support to one another. You will no longer function from a place of self-protection or self-denial; instead, you will be able to show up as authentically yourself, knowing that you are enough and you don't need to protect yourself from or prove yourself to your partner. You accept each other as you are and speak life and truth to each other as you propel each other forward toward growth.

Enneagram Growth Points

1 goes to 7 in growth	4 goes to 1 in growth	7 goes to 5 in growth
2 goes to 4 in growth	5 goes to 8 in growth	8 goes to 2 in growth
3 goes to 6 in growth	6 goes to 9 in growth	9 goes to 3 in growth

Health Points

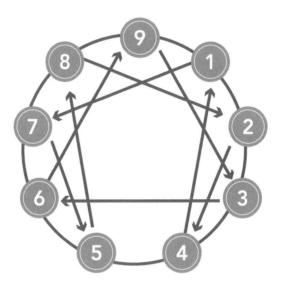

A healthy to average **One** in growth will be able to access the healthy side of a **Seven**. They become less rigid and allow themselves to enjoy freedom, flexibility, and spontaneity. They experience joy and abundance as they release the grip of perfectionism on their life. They begin to see that all they do will be good even if it is not perfect. They learn to go after what they want rather than what they "should" or "must" do. They allow themselves to be curious and open-minded toward new possibilities.

A healthy to average **Two** in growth will be able to access the healthy side of a **Four**. They become more self-accepting and loving toward themselves as well as more honest with themselves about what they are really feeling and thinking. They are able to support others without hoping to get something in return. They are able to have a deeper connection and intimacy with their partner without fear of rejection because they know they have a choice and are not simply waiting to be chosen. They become more authentic, expressive, sensitive, and creative as they feel more grounded in who they are.

A healthy to average **Three** in growth will be able to access the healthy side of a **Six**. They become less competitive and less fearful of failure. They are able to relax and work with their partner toward shared goals and aspirations. They freely offer support and guidance to others as they have learned the value of asking for help when needed. They become more trusting within their relationship and are able to open up emotionally and connect on a heart level.

A healthy to average **Four** in growth will be able to access the healthy side of a **One**. They become more self-accepting. They are able to relax and let go of the constant need for emotional turbulence and crisis in their life. They no longer indulge themselves in hopes of filling the void of not achieving their full potential. They become more objective, grounded, and practical. They desire to get involved in work outside themselves, such as community projects, politics, environmental stewardship, or anything else that seems worthwhile and allows them to engage with their heart and mind.

A healthy to average **Five** in growth will be able to access the healthy side of an **Eight**. They engage in a deeper connection with their partner and no longer fear that they will be overwhelmed by the emotional demands of a relationship. They allow themselves to feel deeply and to become more in touch with their emotions and desires. They become more grounded and confident and are able to speak up for what they want and need. They also step up into a leadership role with courage and wisdom because they know who they are and feel confident within themselves.

A healthy to average **Six** in growth will be able to access the healthy side of a **Nine**. They are able to relax and become less vigilant. They are able to accept life's ups and downs without feeling riddled with anxiety. They no longer second-guess everything because they are learning to trust their inner self and lean into their own wisdom and discernment. They are more serene, grounded, joyous, lighthearted, and stable.

A healthy to average **Seven** in growth will be able to access the healthy side of a **Five**. They are able to quiet their mind and think more clearly. They are able to tap more deeply into their creativity and insight without being scattered. They are also able to follow through with what they are interested in, becoming more productive and satisfied because they are finishing what they start. Their confidence grows as they are able to synthesize information and draw connections. They no longer need constant stimulation but instead look forward to times of quiet solitude when they can realign themselves and rest.

A healthy to average **Eight** in growth will be able to access the healthy side of a **Two**. They become more emotionally in tune and outwardly expressive. They become more generous with their time and resources, understanding that connection is key to healthy relationships. They are able to express how deeply they care for their partner and long to support them. They want to do good and make an impact on the world in a positive way.

A healthy to average **Nine** in growth will be able to access the healthy side of a **Three**. They begin to see themselves as valuable and as having something to contribute to the world. They understand that the peace they seek comes from fully showing up and sharing their gifts and talents with their partner. They begin to invest in themselves because they believe they are worth it. They grow in confidence that they can accomplish what they set their minds to because they feel supported, seen, and heard.

Tips for Each Enneagram Number as They Move toward Growth

Ones find it hard to relax other than when on vacation. To move toward a healthier you, try taking fifteen minutes a day just for yourself. Read, take a walk, listen to music—any activity that allows you to focus on yourself with no outside expectations.

Twos can downplay who they are for the sake of others. As you move toward a healthier you, allow yourself to recognize your own needs. Try not to minimize your needs; instead, share your needs with your partner and allow them to help you meet those needs.

Threes are very driven and believe that they know the best way to achieve a goal. As you move toward a healthier you, allow other people's voices into the conversation. Be willing to shift to others' ideas.

Fours can be intense and sensitive. As you move toward a healthier you, allow yourself to have fun in the process. Find the humor in your everyday life and learn to laugh at yourself and the situations you encounter.

Fives have an uncanny ability to compartmentalize their thoughts from their feelings. As you move toward a healthier you, work on using your body language and emotive words to express how you are feeling.

Sixes can get into the habit of underestimating themselves. They can get caught up in the cycle of negative self-talk. As you move toward a healthier you, take some time and write down positive attributes about yourself. Write down what you like about yourself and what you know you are good at.

Sevens have an overabundance of ideas that are constantly playing in their heads. They can get carried away, talk too much, and overdo in their lives. Moving toward a healthier you, try to listen more than you talk, be mindful of the time, and instead of allowing a new idea to take you off track, stop and work through what is in front of you.

Eights like to be in control. They are capable of moving life forward in a way that does not always allow others to have a voice. As you move toward a healthier version of yourself, take a look at the relationships around you. How much are you leaning on your own strengths and not engaging the strengths of others? Take some time and search yourself to see if you have become more self-focused than relationship-focused.

Nines are known as the sweethearts of the Enneagram. They are the peacemakers, and because of this, they can have a hard time asserting themselves. As you move toward a healthier you, begin to speak up for what you believe in. Be clear about your expectations with kindness but also firmness. You will begin to feel more valued and heard.

Activity

Write your Enneagram number in one of the boxes below and list activities you enjoy that help raise your heart rate and release those much-needed endorphins.

Here's a list to help you get started:

Walking	Hiking	Aerobic class
Running	Rock climbing	Spin class
Cycling	Swimming	Kickboxing
Lifting weights	Dancing	CrossFit

Partner 1	Partner 2

Activity

It is a beautiful thing to be in a relationship where you are celebrated rather than tolerated. In this activity, the circle represents your marriage. Inside this circle, write words, phrases, and activities that honor and celebrate each other. For example:

"You are always so encouraging."

"I love when you dance with me in the kitchen."

"I love when you pray with our children before bed."

"You are such a hard worker, and I appreciate everything you do for our family."

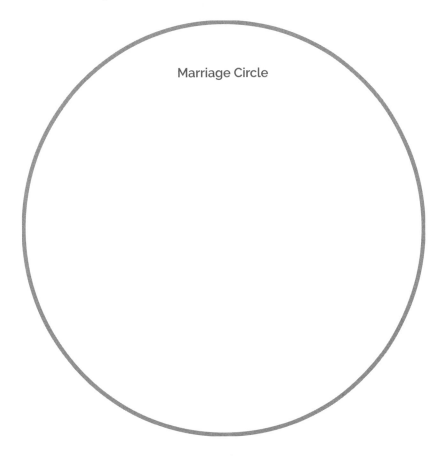

Marriage Circle

Questions

As you review your Enneagram number in health and growth, write down a few words to describe yourself when you are healthy.

Partner 1:

Partner 2:

What healthy rhythms can you establish that will move you toward growth?

Partner 1:

Partner 2:

What disciplines are essential to your health and well-being?

Partner 1:

Partner 2:

What attributes of your partner do you love to see when they are healthy?

Partner 1:

Partner 2:

What words would you love to hear from your partner that help you to see yourself in health and growth?

Partner 1:

Partner 2:

Growing Together through Mutual Compassion and Empathy

Connection and Outlook Groups

> Just when the caterpillar thought the world was over, it became a butterfly.
>
> Anonymous

Healthy marriages are built on love, mutual respect, and trust. Learning how to champion one another is an essential part of growing together rather than apart. When you allow each other to have autonomy and still feel supported and loved, both of you will be able to pursue your purpose and passions with confidence. You will not feel threatened by your partner's success or accomplishments; instead, you will marvel at their growth and achievements.

Professor Barbara Fredrickson, author of *Love 2.0*, asserts that what makes relationships strong "is not big acts of passion, but rather the 'micro-moments of warmth and connection' that happen every hour of every day."[1] You and your partner will not always naturally drift toward each other. You both have to make a concerted effort to connect on a daily basis. Marriage researcher John Gottman found that "taking a few moments to connect with your partner many times every day is essential in building close relationships."[2] Building a close relationship requires both parties to be attentive and interested in each other. Have you heard the phrase "Be around people who celebrate you rather than people who tolerate you"? In your relationship, make it a point to celebrate one another through words and actions. It is important that you can speak words of encouragement to each other and show each other love through your actions. How you respond to each other when you enter a room, send a message, or answer a phone call influences how you feel about the state of your relationship. So it is important that both of you feel celebrated, seen, and validated, not simply tolerated. This will increase emotional connection, intimacy, and a desire to be together.

This week we will dive deeper into our personality types and explore two ways the Enneagram can give you insight into how your childhood patterns of coping and protection have been playing a major role in how you communicate with others. As you learn more about yourself and your patterns, you will begin to identify when you are responding from a posture of defense rather than a place of understanding. You will also learn how to effectively communicate with and support each other as you gain a better understanding of how you each take in and process information through old patterns and beliefs.

Connection-based groups (also called dominant affect groups) are three unconscious emotional states that reveal the childhood background each of us brings to all areas of our lives.[3] The three connection-based groups are *attachment*, *frustration*, and *rejection*.

Connection-based groups are major building blocks of personality. Every person uses all three groups to some degree; however, we each use one as our dominant emotional state. Being aware of your connection-based type can greatly impact transformational work within yourself. With this new awareness, you cannot simply will yourself to change or force yourself to cope or protect differently. Instead, this information enables you to understand where your behavior patterns and thought processes come from. When you know the why behind your behaviors, you can choose to approach situations from a position of understanding rather than correction or shame.

Outlook-based groups (also called harmonic groups) break down how each Enneagram type deals with conflict and disappointment. The three outlook groups are *competency*, *reactive*, and *positive*. According to Riso and Hudson, the harmonic groups tell us how we respond when we do not get what we want. "They reveal the fundamental way that our personality defends against loss and disappointment."[4] These groups will provide an enlightening and helpful perspective for both of you to have as you navigate your relationship over the years.

Connection-Based Groups

Jenna is an Enneagram Six who is loyal and committed to her church. She fell in love with the people and their vision for reaching the city, and she looks forward to Sundays because she volunteers her time in the children's ministry. She also hosts a small group during the week so she can continue to grow in her relationship with the Lord and build community. She loves the conversations that happen around the table at her small group. She is often challenged in a healthy way, and the conversations propel her to spend more time reading her Bible and journaling. But Jenna's fiancé, Nate, does not feel the same way about the church.

Nate is a Five, and he does not love to spend the whole day at church every Sunday. While he enjoys the service and agrees that the people are nice, he doesn't feel the need to get involved at the level Jenna does. Jenna has tried to encourage Nate to be part of a small group or serve in an area that aligns with his interests, but he just dismisses her suggestions. Nate feels like he is being pushed into something he doesn't want to do, which causes him to withdraw and disengage from the entire church experience.

As tension grew within their relationship, they decided to seek help from an Enneagram coach. After several sessions, they realized some of their missed communication had to do with their connection-based groups. Jenna is in the attachment-based group, so she wants to attach to things that bring her comfort and security, such as the church. Nate is in the rejection-based group, so he unconsciously struggles with the belief that he is at the mercy of other people. He expects to be rejected in some way and prefers to keep his circle of friends small and his world private.

As they have gained an understanding of the connection-based groups, Jenna and Nate have been able to give each other space to be who they are. They no longer feel threatened by their different ideas, needs, and opinions. Instead, they've learned to love and support each other with understanding and respect.

· · · · · ·

Attachment-based, frustration-based, and rejection-based groups make up the connection-based groups. These groups unpack the deep-rooted ways each person learned how to keep themselves emotionally safe in childhood. These connection-based groups help to describe each Enneagram type's focus of attention as it pertains to how they interact and function with other people.

The Attachment-Based Group

Threes, Sixes, and Nines make up the attachment-based group. People in this group are focused on relationship and connection to a person or thing that they think helps them maintain their identity. They desire to attach themselves to whatever brings them comfort and provides security—a relationship, a job, a position, their self-image, or even their environment.

- Threes adjust their self-image, feelings, and beliefs in order to be accepted and seen as valuable.
- Sixes defend their relationships, organizations, and institutions because they believe these provide safety and security.
- Nines develop routines, systems, and relationships that bring them freedom, comfort, and peace.

The Frustration-Based Group

Ones, Fours, and Sevens make up the frustration-based group. People in this group struggle with feeling restless, impatient, unfulfilled, and needy.

This stems back to early childhood feelings that their needs were not being fully met. For that reason, people in this group often struggle with feelings of frustration even when their needs are being met, and they can also cause frustration for others as a way to avoid their own feelings. They long to find contentment and fulfillment; however, they can't seem to find what they are looking for, which in turn causes frustration and angst.

- For Ones, frustration mounts when they feel others are not living up to their expectations. They believe that if others lived a life of integrity and acted more orderly, the world would be a better place.
- Fours internalize frustration when they feel like they are not able to create authentically or receive the nurturing and assurance they need from loved ones.
- For Sevens, frustration sets in when the experiences they've been looking and longing for don't fully satisfy them. Because they were expecting these experiences to bring excitement and fulfillment, Sevens often feel disappointed.

The Rejection-Based Group

Twos, Fives, and Eights make up the rejection-based group. People in this group struggle with feeling small, vulnerable, and even weak. They have gone through life expecting to be rejected and therefore have repressed their own need for others' support. Instead, they have tried to protect themselves by being resourceful and helpful. They unconsciously struggle with the belief that they are at the mercy of others. Since they expect to be rejected in some way, they have learned to defend themselves against this feeling.

- For Twos, fear of rejection causes them to work hard at pleasing others so that they will not be tossed aside or abandoned.
- Fives disconnect from their feelings and seek to gather knowledge as a way of protecting themselves from rejection.
- Eights believe they must be powerful and in control so that others do not dare reject them.

The connection-based groups require time, meditation, and self-observation for personal growth and healing. Each person will need to look at what the biggest struggle or false belief is for their Enneagram type and reframe it so they can embrace a new perspective and find balance in their life.

Ones: Allow yourself to acknowledge the beliefs you have around the idea that you are not good enough, that the people around you are not good enough, or that others are not doing things the right way. Growth and healing will happen when you allow yourself to reframe this false belief into the reality of what is true: You are trying your best. You are competent and capable. The people around you view life through a different lens, so while their thoughts and actions may be different from yours, that does not make them bad.

Twos: Allow yourself to acknowledge the beliefs you have around the idea that you are only worth loving if you are doing something for your partner, family, friends, or coworkers. Growth and healing will happen when you allow yourself to reframe this false belief into the reality of what is true: You are worth loving regardless of what you do or give to anyone else. Your self-worth is not found in what other people think about you; instead, it is found in who you are and the value you bring into the relationships.

Threes: Allow yourself to acknowledge the beliefs you have around the idea that you have to perform and be successful for others to value, accept, and love you. Growth and healing will happen when you allow yourself to reframe this false belief into the reality of what is true: Approaching life from a place of authenticity and humility will give you freedom and peace. Giving yourself permission to explore what you are interested in and what you like to do for fun will give you a sense of youthful joy and vibrancy.

Fours: Allow yourself to acknowledge the beliefs you have around the idea that you will never get your needs met in the way you want. Growth and healing will happen when you allow yourself to reframe this false belief into the reality of what is true: You don't need others to meet your needs for you to feel calm and at peace. Instead, allow yourself to take captive runaway thoughts and false beliefs about who you are and your self-worth. Learn to balance your thoughts and emotions by asking yourself, "Is this true?" As you practice this over and over again, you will discover the power to overcome feeling overwhelmed lies within your belief in yourself.

Fives: Allow yourself to acknowledge the beliefs you have around the idea that you must gather resources and knowledge as a way to self-protect and eliminate the need for outside support. Growth and healing will happen when you allow yourself to reframe this false belief into the reality of what is true: You will not be depleted if you invest in healthy, life-giving relationships. Letting yourself be present and engaged with what is happening in and around you will bring a sense of fulfillment and contentment.

Sixes: Allow yourself to acknowledge the beliefs you have around the idea that you have difficulty making decisions apart from outside guidance and support. Growth and healing will happen when you allow yourself to reframe this false belief into the reality of what is true: You are wise, discerning, and courageous. You have the ability to make smart choices apart from other people's opinions.

Sevens: Allow yourself to acknowledge the beliefs you have around the idea that you are not satisfied or getting what you want from life and your relationships. Growth and healing will happen when you allow yourself to reframe this false belief into the reality of what is true: You have everything you need right in front of you. Satisfaction and contentment are found when you turn your attention toward gratitude.

Eights: Allow yourself to acknowledge the beliefs you have around the idea that you have to be strong, bold, and in control of everything and everyone so you will not be hurt, betrayed, or made to look stupid.

Growth and healing will happen when you allow yourself to reframe this false belief into the reality of what is true: You don't always have to assert yourself as a way of self-protection. You can allow yourself to be vulnerable in safe and secure relationships and find connection and contentment.

Nines: Allow yourself to acknowledge the beliefs you have around the idea that your life is best lived going with the flow in hopes of keeping your environment peaceful and harmonious. Growth and healing will happen when you allow yourself to reframe this false belief into the reality of what is true: Doing what you have dreamed about and following through with what you have wanted to do will give you a sense of purpose and fulfillment that you long to feel.

Activity

As you have learned in this week's teaching, relational growth takes awareness of yourself as well as compassion for your partner. Taking time to explore all aspects of yourself and giving your partner space to do the same are so beneficial to the foundation and the depths of your marriage.

In this activity, you will fill in three circles. For the two bottom circles, you and your partner each write the name of your connection-based group on the line above your circle. Inside each of your circles, write what your Enneagram number states about your connection group. In the marriage circle at the top, write the ways you and your partner can support one another with love and compassion.

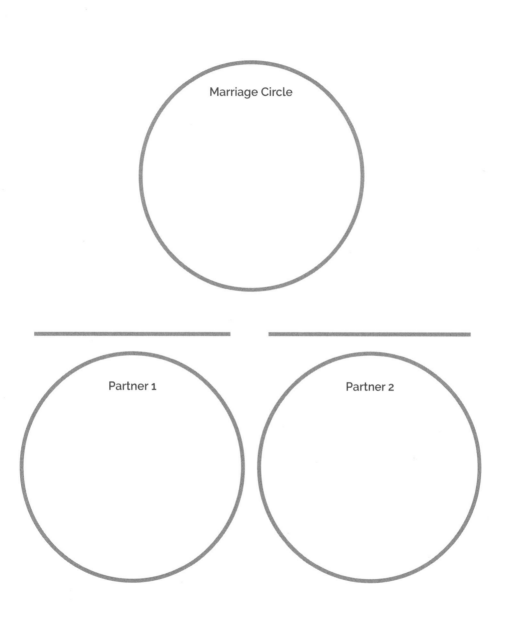

▒▒▒▒ *Questions* ▒▒▒▒

How does the description for your Enneagram number's connection-based group resonate with you?

Partner 1:

Partner 2:

How has your connection-based group helped you in your relationship in the past? How has it hurt you?

Partner 1:

Partner 2:

Write a few sentences stating what you wish your partner knew about you and how you have used your connection-based group to protect yourself through the years.

Partner 1:

Partner 2:

Outlook-Based Groups

Max is an Enneagram Three who is often stoic in the face of emotional situations and prefers to deal with conflict from a logical place. Being goal-oriented, he likes to move at a fast pace and tends to repress his emotions because he feels they get in the way of productivity. Hope, his wife, is a Nine, and she doesn't like conflict and avoids dealing with heavy emotions. This often causes her to not share what is bothering her or show when she is upset. Max and Hope love each other, and they have the same values and vision for their life together. But they avoid hard conversations and are not always willing to speak up when they have been hurt. Instead, they ignore, withdraw, and sometimes even retreat from each other.

As they began to study more about their Enneagram numbers, they realized they are in two different outlook groups. Max is in the competency group. This group deals with difficulties by suppressing their feelings so they can be objective, efficient, and competent. They try to solve problems logically. As a Three, Max focuses on knowing the rules but not being confined by them. He manages his feelings by repressing them, keeping his attention on tasks, and staying busy. Hope is in the positive outlook group, so she responds to conflict by approaching it with a positive attitude. She desires to look at the brighter side of life and enjoys lightening the mood and keeping situations upbeat and conflict-free. Since she tends to focus on the positive and ignore the negative, she struggles with being present and dealing with problems within her relationship and environment.

As Max and Hope have talked through their differences, they have come up with a plan to help them show up emotionally for one another. Because neither of them likes to talk about what makes them frustrated or what has the potential to cause conflict or uncomfortable emotions, they decided to use a candle as a way to start a conversation. Max and Hope bought a candle and placed it on the mantel in their living room. When one of them lights the candle, that means they want to talk about something. This gives them a common signal that they need to have a conversation and enables them to bring up a topic in a less confrontational way. They also start these conversations with "The story I am telling myself is . . ." Max and Hope have found this approach helpful and less scary. They both desire to work on emotional connection and to love, honor, and respect each other. This new system has helped them find a new rhythm within their relationship that has permitted them to speak the truth in love.

. . . . . .

You and your partner can find a healthy rhythm to communicate your thoughts, feelings, and frustrations using the knowledge you will gain from the outlook groups. These groups provide stability and awareness that allows for deeper work of self-discovery. As you learn more about yourself and your partner through the outlook groups, you will have an opportunity to practice strategies that will help you become grounded and centered. You will both learn about your coping strategies and be able to understand the reasons you do what you do. You will see that each of you is more than your Enneagram type and your patterns of behavior because you will understand that these are the ways you have learned how to cope through your lives. Both of you will be able to embrace who you are and see how you have been perfectly crafted. You are both beautiful from the inside out. You both will be able to reside fully in your being because you have learned to ground yourself in what is real and true instead of functioning from your autopilot of protection. Both of you will be filled with joy and contentment and will be able to discern what is right without being overwhelmed or fearful. Understanding yourselves through the outlook groups has the potential to change the trajectory of your relationship because it offers awareness and gives you words to describe how you learned to cope and protect yourself.

The Competency Group

Ones, Threes, and Fives make up the competency group. People in this group deal with difficulties by suppressing their feelings so they can be objective, efficient, and competent. They try to solve problems logically. This group struggles to work within systems. They don't want to give themselves over to a system fully, nor do they want to abandon the system completely.

- Ones focus on obeying the rules, improving themselves, and being correct and organized. They manage their feelings by getting involved in an activity and doing things perfectly, and they tend to be inflexible.
- Threes focus on knowing the rules without being confined by them, and by being efficient, focused, goal-oriented, and pragmatic. They manage their feelings by repressing them and keeping their attention on tasks and staying busy.
- Fives focus on operating outside the rules by gathering facts and data and becoming experts. They manage their feelings by compartmentalizing and staying preoccupied.

The Reactive Group

Fours, Sixes, and Eights make up the reactive group. People in this group react emotionally to conflict and problems. When problems do occur, they look for an emotional response that mirrors their concerns, whether that is happy, angry, excited, or perhaps even grief-stricken. In conflict they need to deal with their own feelings first, and they often look to the other person in hopes that they will match their emotional state.

- Fours focus on being seen, supported, understood, and perhaps even rescued. Fear causes them to believe they will be abandoned, uncared for, neglected, and left to figure life out on their own.
- Sixes focus on being independent, but they also desire support and stability. Fear causes them to become scared of losing support

but also of being too reliant on someone else and losing their autonomy.

- Eights focus on independence, self-reliance, and provision, hoping to minimize their needs as much as possible. Fear of being too vulnerable or exposed causes them to become controlling, suspicious, and withdrawn.

The Positive Group

Twos, Sevens, and Nines make up the positive outlook group. The people in this group respond to conflict by approaching it with a positive attitude. They desire to look at the brighter side of life. They enjoy lightening the mood and keeping situations upbeat.

This group struggles to look at the darker side of themselves and others. They avoid emotions, conversations, and encounters that could cause conflict in any way they can.

- Twos focus on the needs of others and their own good intentions. They avoid their own needs, disappointment, and feelings of anger.
- Sevens focus on their own needs as well as positive experiences, adventure, and fun. They avoid their role in creating pain and suffering for themselves or others.
- Nines ignore their own needs and elevate the needs of others and the positive qualities they see in people and their environment. They avoid being present and dealing with problems within their relationships and environment.

Below are a few suggestions to help you lower your defenses and better connect with your partner according to your outlook group. Using the knowledge about how you have learned to cope and keep disappointment at bay through the outlook groups can help you drop your guard and allow your partner closer to enable a deeper, more meaningful emotional connection.

Ones: Seek peace of mind by allowing yourself to acknowledge what you are feeling and how it is affecting your behavior. Make a point of not holding on to frustrations and resentment. By being honest with yourself and your partner about what you are feeling and why you are feeling this way, you open yourself up for connection and comfort.

Twos: Seek mental freedom and tranquility as you allow your repressed needs to surface and hidden frustrations to be revealed. Allow yourself to share your feelings of fear, sadness, and rejection with your partner, trusting they will bring you comfort and peace.

Threes: Seek to open your heart and allow yourself to acknowledge what you are feeling. Give yourself permission to admit feelings of inadequacy and shame. Allow your partner to share in the experience so they can comfort you and speak words of love and acceptance to you.

Fours: Seek to ground yourself in truth. Allow yourself to see where your thinking has become distorted and your self-image has been skewed. Invite your partner into the process by sharing "The story I have been telling myself is . . ." and accept the comfort and love they seek to give you.

Fives: Seek to anchor yourself in your body and allow yourself to grieve feelings of rejection and hopelessness. Try sharing your thoughts and fears with your partner, and receive the support and love they are willing to share with you.

Sixes: Seek to cultivate a quiet mind and recognize what is true and what is fear-based thinking that causes anxiety and a quick temper. Allow your partner to help you process your thoughts and speak truth to bring you comfort and peace.

Sevens: Seek to open yourself up and allow blocked energy around repressed feelings of sadness and regret to be released. Invite your partner into the process and share with them what you are afraid of and what you need, allowing them to give you comfort and peace.

Eights: Seek to be honest and vulnerable with yourself as you explore your familiar patterns and thought processes around fear and weakness. Invite your partner to the conversations you are having in your mind and allow them to bring comfort, truth, and stability.

Nines: Seek to root yourself in understanding and self-acceptance, allowing yourself to release repressed anger and fear that have been blocked in you. Allow your partner to hear what you have been holding on to and permit them to speak words of life and truth over you.

As you learn to lower your defenses and be more open, your connection with one another will grow and mature. You will find it easier to be vulnerable and open. It is crucial that you and your partner each do your own work of self-awareness so that you both feel accepted and loved, not forced to conform because that is what is expected of you. Growth is both personal and collaborative. It is so beneficial to have a trusted partner who can speak the truth in love and help you see yourself in a healthy way.

Activity

This activity has three circles. On the lines above the two bottom circles, you and your partner each write the name of your outlook-based group. Inside your circle, write what your Enneagram number states about your outlook group. In the marriage circle at the top, write the ways you are willing to help your partner move toward growth as they see things about their patterns that are not giving them the results they desire.

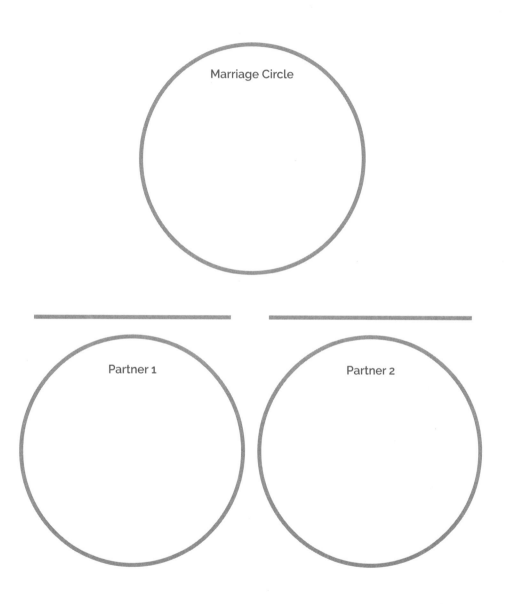

Marriage Circle

Partner 1

Partner 2

▬▬ *Questions* ▬▬

How does the description for your Enneagram number's outlook group resonate with you?

Partner 1:

Partner 2:

Rewrite your outlook group description in your own words.

Partner 1:

Partner 2:

What is a new piece of awareness you have learned about your partner as you have read through their outlook group description?

Partner 1:

Partner 2:

What is one way you can support your partner with the new awareness you are gaining about them?

Partner 1:

Partner 2:

. . . . . .

We'll close this chapter with a visual tool that can teach you ways to show up emotionally in your relationship.

Become aware of: Take notice of what is happening with your partner. What do you think they are feeling or thinking?

Try to make sense: What fear is being triggered? What need is not being met? What desire is trying to be expressed?

Respond: Make eye contact and turn your body toward your partner. Ask questions and allow your partner to express himself or herself. Move toward your partner for comfort and support. Remember, your partner wants to be heard, not fixed, and seen, not silenced, so make sure your posture is open and engaging.

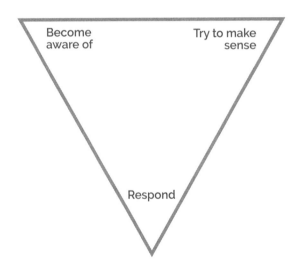

Conclusion

As I said at the beginning of this journey, you and your partner are both unique individuals who see the world from different perspectives. The goal of this workbook has been to help you and your partner gain self-awareness and a deeper understanding of your patterns of behavior and the ways in which you each view the world. I hope it has helped you form a deeper bond through empathy, compassion, and connection. This workbook was not created as a tool to help you "win" an argument. Instead, my hope is that you have learned how to understand each other in a way that allows you both to feel safe and secure within the relationship. As the two of you grow in emotional connection, you will begin to think about the decisions and situations you face with a "we" mindset instead of a "me" mindset. You will ask "How will this decision affect us?" instead of "How will this decision affect me?"

As you learn to communicate with each other in kind, gentle, and understanding tones, you will want to protect your relationship. You will feel deeply connected, cherished, and supported, and this will prompt you to build healthy boundaries to ensure you are protecting your family. Make a point of speaking words of encouragement to each other. Point out the things you love about each other, and try to connect often in physical ways such as a hug, kiss, warm touch, or intimacy. The more you respond to each other's bids for connection, the more you will feel drawn to each other.

You need each other for support, connection, love, intimacy, and partnership. So lean in and love each other with the new awareness you have gained from all the hard work you have done in this workbook. Whether this is the start of your life together or you picked up this workbook somewhere along your journey, building your relationship on a solid foundation is the key to deep, lasting connection and meaningful communication.

Let's conclude *The Enneagram and Your Marriage* with two last activities. These will require you and your partner to look back through your notes to fill in the circles and squares.

Activity

The circles on the facing page represent you and your partner and your marriage. You and your spouse each have your own circle in which to write down what you need to keep yourselves healthy, strong, and connected. Examples of things you could write include prayer, exercise, eight hours of sleep, time with friends, alone time, time for a hobby, and so on. You are responsible for filling your circle with what you need in order to not only survive but thrive in your life.

The marriage circle at the top will be filled out by both of you. You will each put one foot in the marriage circle while leaving your other foot in your personal circle. You never step into your partner's circle by trying to fix them or by giving them what you think they need. Instead, in the marriage circle, you give to each other out of an overflow of who you are. If you have been doing your own personal work, you will have the patience, margin, and ability to love your partner the way they need to be loved, not simply the way you need to be loved. In the marriage circle, write down what you need from one another. Examples include quality time, affection, the ability to listen without interrupting, support, guidance, tenderness, and so on.

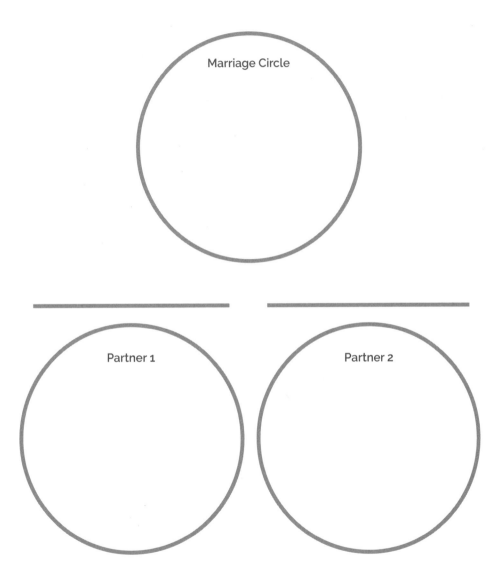

▬▬▬ *Activity* ▬▬▬

The squares below are a guide to help you and your partner write out your goals, hopes, dreams, and vision for how you see your relationship functioning and not functioning.

In the large outer square, write down all the ways you both would like your relationship to function. This is the healthy outer layer.

In the middle square, write down those things you are okay with sometimes, or perhaps those things you want to have a say in ahead of time. Examples include girls' trips, guys' nights out, spending money, extra hobbies, and so forth.

In the inner square, write your absolute nos. These are the things you will not tolerate in the relationship.

After you have filled in the squares, write consequences for violating the absolute nos to establish healthy boundaries. If there is not a clear consequence, there is not a clear boundary.

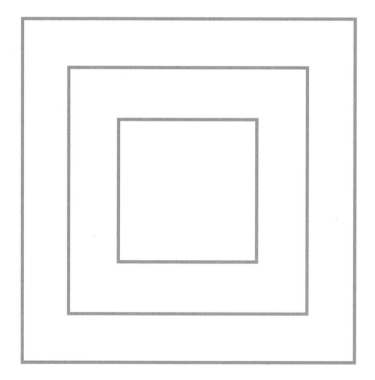

. . . . . .

These two activities have helped you and your partner establish what is healthy and beneficial for each of you within your relationship. Keep this book in an accessible place where you can revisit often. Adjust your circles and squares as your relationship grows and changes. Relationships require constant work and movement. You will not naturally drift toward each other, so be intentional with your words and actions.

Congratulations to both of you for investing in your relationship and allowing yourselves to take a deep dive into your personality types, patterns of behavior, and vulnerable places. You both will continue to grow as you put into practice the information you have learned over the past seven weeks. You will feel a sense of peace knowing you now have a better understanding and a solid foundation on which to continue building your relationship. The work you have done over the past seven weeks is just like the ductwork my family had to replace underneath our home. Establishing a solid foundation underneath our home allowed us to relax, be at peace, and breathe easier.

My hope for you both as you continue on your marriage journey is that you would move toward each other for connection and continue to pursue each other as you uncover and discover more about one another through the years. Enjoy the journey and each other.

Appendix A

Narrative Approach Quick Test

The Narrative Approach to the Enneagram, developed by Helen Palmer in the early 1970s, allows you to explore each Enneagram type in a more open and personal way.[1] Using this approach allows you to question your own patterns of behavior and look at the root cause or motivation behind why you do what you do. This short narrative test is a great starting point to discover your Enneagram type.

After you complete this test, turn back to week 1 and read the description for your resulting number. Then read the descriptions of the other Enneagram numbers, keeping an open mind and allowing yourself to see what truly resonates. Take note of the unconscious childhood message (week 2) and childhood longing (week 3) for your Enneagram number and ask yourself, "Does this message hit home?" and "Does this longing stir something in me that feels both comforting and exposing?"

As you go through this workbook, you will begin to resonate with one number more than all the other numbers. It is important to remember that your Enneagram number does not change throughout your life. Your Enneagram number is rooted in your heart longing message, which causes you to create patterns of behavior in an effort to receive love, keep yourself safe, and get your needs met.

Directions for the Narrative Approach Quick Test

First, read the paragraphs in part 1 and choose the one that feels most like you. Second, read the paragraphs in part 2 and choose the one that feels most like you. Next, take the shape from part 1 that you most resonate with and the shape from part 2 that you most resonate with and put them next to each other. Look at the key on page 194 and find the Enneagram number that matches that combination. Then turn back to week 1 and read more about your number and begin to explore it with an open mind.

Part 1

I tend to be independent and assertive, maybe even aggressive at times. I have always set my sights on what I want and have gone after it with passion and gusto. I don't like other people telling me what to do or how to do it. I prefer to be the one who makes the plan, and I want to be involved in executing the plan. I don't want to sit around; instead, I like to make things happen. I really feel like my life is meant to have an impact on the world and there are important things for me to do. I don't necessarily like confrontation, but I am not afraid of it. I don't let people push me around; instead, I stand up for what I feel is important. I usually know what I want, and I go after it with confidence. I am a hard worker as well as a playful and fun person.

I tend to be quiet and more reserved. I don't assert myself often, nor am I a very social person. I can fly under the radar because I don't like to draw attention to myself or take the lead. I am not very competitive. I spend a lot of time dreaming and thinking about new possibilities of what could be. My imagination is lively, so I don't feel the need to be active all the time. I enjoy my own space and my alone time.

I feel a great deal of responsibility to do what is expected of me. I am a very responsible person who feels deeply for others. People really matter to me, so I always want to be known as someone who thinks of others and has their best interests at heart. I can be self-sacrificing at times because I think about others above myself. Many times people don't realize the sacrifices I have made for them. I tend to put my needs, wants, and desires last. I am always trying to do what needs to be done first, and if there's time, I will allow myself to relax.

Part 2

I am typically upbeat and happy. I have a positive outlook on life and often look for the silver lining in every situation. I am a social person who uses enthusiasm and excitement to help people feel better and see all the possibilities that lie ahead. I like to stay busy and enjoy sharing my life and experiences with others. I don't want to share my difficulties and hardships, so sometimes I prolong my own ability to process and heal.

I don't like to be told what to do. I know the ways things are supposed to go, but I don't want people telling me what to do. I feel things strongly, and most people can sense when I am not okay. I am very sensitive, but others don't usually realize just how sensitive I am. I keep my guard up because I don't like to be vulnerable, nor do I want to end up in a situation where I am unclear of where I stand. However, most people know where they stand with me. I feel things deeply, and I look for others to validate my feelings and to get as worked up as I am.

I am a logical thinker who prefers not to bring feelings into situations. I am uncomfortable with emotions and can easily feel overwhelmed, which causes me to retreat or withdraw. I try to stay composed when conflict arises because I don't like when emotions distract from the issue at hand. I like to work alone, and I am very efficient, disciplined, and sometimes even perfectionistic. Others say I am calm, cool, and at times even detached or distant.

★	▲	7 The Energetic Enthusiast
★	⬡	8 The Protective Challenger
★	◼	3 The Determined Achiever
●	▲	9 The Peaceful Mediator
⬤	⬡	4 The Romantic Individualist
●	◼	5 The Investigative Thinker
♥	▲	2 The Supportive Advisor
♥	⬡	6 The Friendly Loyalist
♥	◻	1 The Moral Perfectionist

Appendix B

Levels of Health

Levels of health within the Enneagram system are designed to inform you of when you are functioning from a healthy, average, or unhealthy place. To live your life in the healthy range you must be intentional to acknowledge your patterns of behavior. When you are grounded in who you are and understand your worth comes from the Lord, you can live authentically. You show Christ to the world through your kindness, generosity, and love.

You may find yourself in the average range and wonder how you went from healthy to average. Well, when fear and worry enter the picture, you begin to use your coping strategies and past patterns of behavior. Each Enneagram number in the average range tries to protect their heart longing message by doing what they believe will keep them safe, get their needs met, and gain love and acceptance.

If you find yourself in the unhealthy range, it is because the stressors of life have overridden you and you are using what you know to survive. You have likely lost sight of your true value and have turned to your signature sin to help you cope. You are overwhelmed and exhausted and most likely feel alone in your struggle.

Keep in mind that you can fluctuate between these levels from day to day, week to week, and season to season. The point of understanding the levels of health is for you to recognize where you are and what has caused you to get there. You are never stuck in a level. You always have the choice to acknowledge, change, heal, and grow. You will need your partner to help you along the way. So lean in and learn about yourself and allow your partner to love you even when you feel unlovable.

Levels of Health for ONES
Healthy

- composed
- critically aware
- ethical

Average

- perfectionistic
- thorough
- flattering

Unhealthy

- pretentious
- self-righteous
- corrosive

Levels of Health for TWOS
Healthy

- caring
- friendly
- sensitive

Average

- maternal/paternal
- generous
- helping

Unhealthy

- manipulative
- controlling
- codependent

Levels of Health for THREES
Healthy

- truthful
- competent
- reliable

Average

- image-conscious
- pragmatic
- positioning

Unhealthy

- opportunistic
- deceptive
- self-seeking

Levels of Health for FOURS
Healthy

- authentic
- disciplined
- creative

Average

- romantic
- unique
- introspective

Unhealthy

- depressed
- self-indulgent
- clingy

Levels of Health for FIVES

Healthy

- pioneering
- wise
- energetic

Average

- analytical
- distanced
- abstract

Unhealthy

- isolated
- eccentric
- rebellious

Levels of Health for SIXES

Healthy

- loyal
- courageous
- confident

Average

- dutiful
- careful
- antiauthoritarian

Unhealthy

- clingy
- anxious
- irritable

Levels of Health for SEVENS

Healthy

- happy
- accomplished
- calm

Average

- hyperactive
- superficial
- distracted

Unhealthy

- excessive
- opinionated
- reactive

Levels of Health for EIGHTS

Healthy

- generous
- protective
- leadership-minded

Average

- controlling
- direct
- competitive

Unhealthy

- domineering
- authoritarian
- rebellious

Levels of Health for NINES

Healthy

- accepting
- peacemaking
- goal-oriented

Average

- compliant
- indecisive
- easygoing

Unhealthy

- melancholy
- stubborn
- bewildered

Appendix C

Creating a Value System

Brad and Shannon have been married for just over four years and are blessed with two beautiful daughters, Ella and Kate. The girls are only fourteen months apart, so life is full of diapers, feedings, crying, and messes. Brad and Shannon never really discussed what they wanted the value system of their home to be. They knew they had grown up in very different homes and that because of this they didn't always see eye to eye on marriage and parenting issues. But they just figured this was life and they would make the best of it.

You see, Brad is a Five who grew up in a single-parent home. His mother was a hardworking woman who always had time to listen to Brad and his brothers tell stories of what happened during their school day or who got in a fight with whom. His mother instilled the importance of loving people well and looking out for those less fortunate. She had a laugh that could be heard a mile away and a smile that would light up the darkest of souls. She was full of kindness and love, and she often looked the other way or ignored the situation when the boys behaved poorly. Their home valued empathy, love, generosity, and laughter.

Shannon, an Eight, grew up in a very different home. Her parents owned a successful business and often spent long hours at the office. They put a lot of emphasis on good grades and achievements. Shannon and her sister both participated in sports and had to learn to play a musical instrument.

They knew how important it was to strive to be the best at everything they did. Her parents were very strict, and there was always a consequence for a poor action. Still, Shannon's parents loved her and her sister very much, and they showed this by taking them on great trips and buying them nice things. Shannon learned to value success, achievement, the finer things, and traditional family values.

You can imagine the conflict and confusion Brad and Shannon felt as they each tried to assert their own family's value systems into their new marriage and family. They had plenty of heated discussions and more than their fair share of miscommunication throughout their four years of marriage, until one day they sat down and worked on coming up with what they wanted the value system of their home to look like. Together they merged parts of their individual upbringing and infused them with some new ideas. They came up with a value system they felt represented who they are today and how they envision their home to be. They put together a chart of things that were important for their family, including eating dinner together, reading bedtime stories to the kids, letting laughter fill their home, teaching their children to give generously, sticking with what you started, date nights, family camping trips, a personal relationship with Christ, and so much more.

Like all people, you have grown up learning to either accept or fight against the value system that was established within your childhood home or environment. It doesn't matter if you were raised in a two-parent home, a single-parent home, your grandparents' home, a family friend's home, a foster home, or a group home—all those environments have a value system that establishes how you experience love, acceptance, care, safety, and security. You might have grown up in a home or environment where you did not feel protected or loved. But even in that home there was a value system: If you achieve and perform, you earn your place within the family. If you give generously and support others, you are praised and accepted. If you toe the line and do what is right, you are affirmed. You get the picture. Your parents or caretakers were influenced by their own upbringings. They either continued to value what they had learned or did the opposite of what they had experienced to create an environment based on the value systems they deemed important.

Often value systems within marriages and families are not discussed; they are simply acted upon and become the unspoken rules about the way in which the home functions. You end up bringing the value system you learned from childhood into your marriage relationship and expect your partner to live up to or receive love, acceptance, and affection based on this value system, even if you have never discussed it. It is so vital to establish a healthy value system that you and your partner both agree on. It is important that each of you has an equal voice in establishing your value system so that your marriage and family function in a healthy and united way.

Establishing your value system will require honesty and respect. As you talk out what you envision your marriage and home to feel like and look like, be mindful that you have come from completely different homes. Learning to merge together will take time and clear communication, but it will be worth it because you will become much more unified if you are willing to listen to and respect each other.

Activity

On the next page, fill in the middle circle with your family vision statement. Here are some examples:

"Our family is adventurous, kind, and considerate, and we love to laugh a lot."

"Our family will pursue our purpose with passion and consistency. We will finish what we start and speak with respect."

"Our family will love, honor, and respect one another."

In the small circles that are connected to the main circle, write down the ways your family will accomplish the vision statement. Here are a few examples:

"We will speak kindly to one another."

"We will support one another's dreams."

"We will stick to what we start."

"We will be generous with our resources."

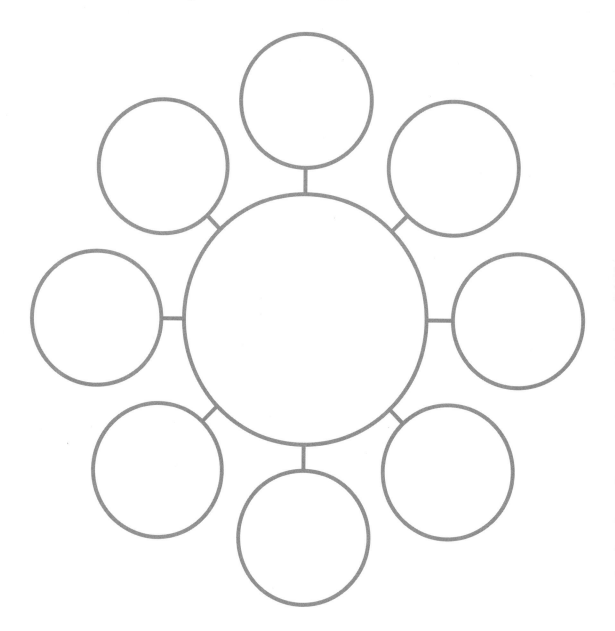

Acknowledgments

I t is my joy and passion to bring Enneagram awareness and practical application to my audience. There have been many family members and friends who have championed me in this endeavor. I am so thankful for Jenny Acuff who sent me my first Enneagram book, *The Wisdom of the Enneagram*. This book propelled me down the path I find myself walking today. Thank you to my mother, Kathy Goetsch, and my sister, Jennifer Moore, for believing in me and letting me talk nonstop about the Enneagram. Thank you to my many friends—Brandi Wilson, Lindsey Nobles, Julie Cannon, Eve Annunziato, Logan Raines, and so many others—who saw a passion burning inside of me and pushed me toward it. Thank you to Ali Lopes for your amazing design talents and friendship. You have truly helped people visualize what I want to convey. Thank you to Becky Brewster for your hard work and dedication on this project. You are a gift to me and I am so thankful for you. And, of course, a huge thank-you to my husband, Stephen Brewster, for supporting and believing in me, as well as to my children: Isaiah, Ashlyn, Hope, and Grace. I love you more than words could ever say.

I'd like to acknowledge the many great Enneagram teachers who have paved the path for me and so many others to uncover and discover more about ourselves. They are trailblazers who have propelled so many individuals on their personal journey of awareness, healing, and growth. So a huge thank-you to Russ Hudson, Don Riso, Beth McCord, Richard Rohr, Suzanne Stabile, Beatrice Chestnut, Marilyn Vancil, and so many others.

A huge thank-you to Patnacia Goodman and Amy Nemecek along with the team at Baker Books for seeing the value in this book and helping to craft a tool that delivers life transformation and healing.

Notes

Week 1 Building the Foundation

1. Richard Rohr, *The Enneagram: A Christian Perspective* (New York: The Crossroad Publishing Company, 2019), 3.

2. Don Richard Riso and Russ Hudson, *The Wisdom of the Enneagram* (New York: Bantam Books, 1999), 24.

3. Riso and Hudson, *Wisdom of the Enneagram*, 24.

4. Beatrice Chestnut, *The Complete Enneagram: 27 Paths to Greater Self-Knowledge* (Berkeley, CA: She Writes Press, 2013), 12.

5. The names assigned to each wing come from Don Richard Riso and Russ Hudson, *Personality Types: Using the Enneagram for Self-Discovery* (New York: Houghton Mifflin, 1996).

6. Quoted in Mike Parkinson, "The Power of Visual Communication," excerpted from his book *Do-It-Yourself Billion Dollar Graphics* (n.p.: PepperLip Press, 2010), https://innovative researchmethods.org/wp-content/uploads/2020/10/The-Power-of-Visual-Communication_Parkinson.pdf.

Week 2 Breaking Down Barriers

1. Don Richard Riso and Russ Hudson, *The Wisdom of the Enneagram* (New York: Bantam Books, 1999), 31.

2. Riso and Hudson, *Wisdom of the Enneagram*, 31.

3. Riso and Hudson, *Wisdom of the Enneagram*, 31.

4. Sue Johnson, *Love Sense: The Revolutionary New Science of Romantic Relationships* (New York: Little, Brown Spark, 2013), 86.

5. Quoted in Lisa Firestone, "Are You the Pursuer or the Distancer in Your Relationship?," *Psychology Today*, April 21, 2017, https://www.psychologytoday.com/us/blog/compassion-matters/201704/are-you-the-pursuer-or-the-distancer-in-your-relationship.

6. For more on this, see Daniel J. Siegel and Tina Payne Bryson, *The Power of Showing Up* (New York: Ballantine Books, 2020).

7. Johnson, *Love Sense*, 86.

8. Mia Belle Frothingham, "Fight, Flight, Freeze, or Fawn: What This Response Means," Simply Psychology, October 6, 2021, https://www.simplypsychology.org/fight-flight-freeze-fawn.html.

Week 3 Growing Together through Communication and Connection

1. Don Richard Riso and Russ Hudson, *The Wisdom of the Enneagram* (New York: Bantam Books, 1999), 32.
2. Saul McLeod, "Id, Ego, and Superego," Simply Psychology, September 25, 2019, https://www.simplypsychology.org/psyche.html.
3. Sharon Martin, "Why Do We Repeat the Same Dysfunctional Relationship Patterns Over and Over?," PsychCentral, July 13, 2018, https://psychcentral.com/blog/imperfect/2018/07/why-do-we-repeat-the-same-dysfunctional-relationship-patterns.
4. Riso and Hudson, *Wisdom of the Enneagram*, 34.

Week 4 Leveling Up

1. Beatrice Chestnut, *The Complete Enneagram: 27 Paths to Greater Self-Knowledge* (Berkeley, CA: She Writes Press, 2013), 18.
2. Don Richard Riso and Russ Hudson, *The Wisdom of the Enneagram* (New York: Bantam Books, 1999), 55.
3. Brené Brown, *Atlas of the Heart* (New York: Random House, 2021), 137.
4. Riso and Hudson, *Wisdom of the Enneagram*, 57.
5. American Psychological Association, "Anxiety," https://www.apa.org/topics/anxiety.
6. Riso and Hudson, *Wisdom of the Enneagram*, 53.
7. Brown, *Atlas of the Heart*, 220.
8. Riso and Hudson, *Wisdom of the Enneagram*, 23.

Week 5 Overcoming Pitfalls

1. Don Richard Riso and Russ Hudson, *The Wisdom of the Enneagram* (New York: Bantam Books, 1999), 23.

Week 6 Building a Solid Connection through Security and Love

1. Adam Felman, "What Is Good Health?," Medical News Today, updated April 19, 2020, https://www.medicalnewstoday.com/articles/150999.

Week 7 Growing Together through Mutual Compassion and Empathy

1. Pat LaDouceur, "Drifting Apart and How to Reconnect," MentalHelp.net, https://www.mentalhelp.net/blogs/drifting-apart-and-how-to-reconnect/.
2. LaDouceur, "Drifting Apart."
3. Don Richard Riso and Russ Hudson, *Understanding the Enneagram* (Boston: Houghton Mifflin, 2000), 315.
4. Don Richard Riso and Russ Hudson, *The Wisdom of the Enneagram* (New York: Bantam Books, 1999), 64.

Appendix A Narrative Approach Quick Test

1. The Narrative Enneagram, "About Us," accessed May 11, 2022, https://www.narrativeenneagram.org/about-us/.

Jackie Brewster is a certified Enneagram coach and a certified experiential specialist. She lives in Franklin, Tennessee, with her husband, Stephen, and their four amazing children. She helps individuals, teams, and organizations overcome being overwhelmed. Jackie focuses on helping people uncover and discover who they are and how to grow toward health in their personal lives as well as in their corporate roles through the teachings of the Enneagram and biblical truths.